THE IRISH CULTURE BOOK 2

STUDENT BOOK

by

IAN O'MALLEY

978-1-326-13028-2

Published by Malleyman Publications, Dublin, 2017.

TABLE OF CONTENTS

ALL LISTENING EXTRACTS CAN BE DOWNLOADED FOR FREE AT:
www.irishculturebook.com

MAP OF THE BOOK

UNIT 1 **QUESTIONS** **ABOUT IRELAND** **Page 11**	**Warm Up / Quotes Section** **Part 1 Around the World** *Match facts & countries* **Part 2 Twenty Questions** *Test your Knowledge* **On Your Own**	***Main Discussion Areas*** *Facts about different countries* *Facts about Ireland* ***Follow-on Activities*** *Make your own 'country quiz'*
UNIT 2 **IRISH SPORT** **Page 19**	**Warm Up / Quotes Section** **Part 1 'Faster…'** *Match & describe Olympic sports* **Part 2 Gaelic Games** *Quiz & reading comprehension* **Part 2B Legend of Hurling** *Read & discuss* **Part 3A/3B Sporting Greats** *Match & identify* **Part 4A Sporting Moment** *Read, watch & discuss* **On Your Own**	***Main Discussion Areas*** *Olympic sports* *Importance of Gaelic games* *Irish & international sportspeople* *Sport & Irish history/politics* ***Follow-on Activities*** *Invent your own sports* *Watch or play an Irish sport*
UNIT 3 **IRISH** **CHARACTER &** **RELATIONSHIPS** **Page 23**	**Warm Up / Quotes Section** **Part 1A National Character** *Discussing stereotypes* **Part 1B 'I'd like to…'** *Write a short poem* **Part 2A What do you…?** *Rank the characteristics* **Part 2B/2C Romance/Dating** *Compare cultures* **Part 2D 'Where do…?'** *Order the relationship stages* **Part 3A/3B 'Funny Thing…'** *Matching humour types* **Part 3C Irish Humour** *Reading comprehension* **Part 4A 'Tá mé…'** *Rank the love expressions* **Part 4B Love Languages** *Love questionnaire* **Part 4C Forbidden Love** *Predict end of story* **On Your Own**	***Main Discussion Areas*** *National 'self-stereotypes'* *Meeting new people* *Romance, dating & relationships* *Humour in different cultures* *Love stories* ***Follow-on Activities*** *Watch some Irish comedy* *Find some jokes in English* *Find out about romance in Ireland*
UNIT 4 **SCIENCE,** **INNOVATION** **& BUSINESS** **Page 27**	**Warm Up / Quotes Section** **Part 1 World Inventions** *Matching & rating* **Part 2A Irish Inventions** *Matching & ordering* **Part 2B Gulliver's Travels** *Survival game* **Part 3A Science Quiz** *Answer the questions* **Part 3B Irish Invented Wind** *Invent a scale* **Part 4A/4B World Business** *Etiquette Quiz* **On Your Own**	***Main Discussion Areas*** *Inventions & inventiveness* *Science* *Economics & business etiquette* ***Follow-on Activities*** *Create your own inventions* *Visit science museum*
UNIT 5 **VISUAL IRELAND** **Page 31**	**Warm Up / Quotes Section** **Part 1 Art History** *Art history & awareness* **Part 2A/2B Architecture** *Matching & evaluating* **Part 2C Houses** *Thinking about design* **Part 3A/3B Image/Fashion** *Identify & evaluate* **Part 3C Colour** *Personality quiz* **Part 4 Painting** *Match, discuss & evaluate* **On Your Own**	***Main Discussion Areas*** *Early Irish art history* *Architectural styles in Ireland* *Irish fashion* *Modern Irish painting* ***Follow-on Activities*** *Design a fashion outfit* *Design a city/house*
UNIT 6 **IRISH MYTHS** **& LEGENDS** **Page 35**	**Warm Up / Quotes Section** **Part 1 Characters** *Match descriptions* **Part 2A Irish Heroes** *Read & compare* **Part 2B Legend Themes** *Link old & new* **Part 3A/3B Otherworld** *Discuss & reflect* **Part 4/5 'Labhraidh/Lir/Oisín'** *Read & match* **On Your Own**	***Main Discussion Areas*** *Typical legend characters/themes* *Modern day legends & heroes* *Irish legends* ***Follow-on Activities*** *Visit ancient legendary sites* *Invent your own legend* *Read Irish mythology*

MAP OF THE BOOK *CONTD.*

UNIT 7 **HOW IRISH** **SPEAK** **Page 35**	**Warm Up / Quotes Section** **Part 1 Accents** *Tongue twister* **Part 2 Around the World** *Identify colloquial English* **Part 3A Old & Middle** *Getting meaning from context* **Part 3B 'As Gaeilge'** *Comparing languages* **Part 3C Correct the Mistakes** *Irish constructions* **Part 4A/4B 'I'm grand'** *Irish expressions* **Part 5 'That's lovely'** *Expanding vocabulary* **On Your Own**	***Main Discussion Areas*** *Understanding accents* *Improving pronunciation* *Colloquial language* *Features of Irish-English* *Irish character in language* ***Follow-on Activities*** *Research regional variations* *Record your own pronunciation*
UNIT 8 **HOW IRISH MOVE** **Page 39**	**Warm Up / Quotes Section** **Part 1 Gestures Quiz** *Test your cultural knowledge* **Part 2A Non-Verbal** *Read & answer* **Part 2B Interjections** *Match sounds & meaning* **Part 3A 'Dance like…'** *Matching. Choose adjectives* **Part 4 What type…?** *Learning style questionnaire* **Part 5 Irish Dancing** *Reading comprehension* **On Your Own**	***Main Discussion Areas*** *Gestures & body language* *Cultural communication* *Irish dancing* ***Follow-on Activities*** *Physical games in classroom* *Do some Irish dancing*
UNIT 9 **IRISH FILM** **Page 43**	**Warm Up / Quotes Section** **Part 1 Irish Actors** *Match actor, role & film* **Part 2A/2B Movies** *Match genres & descriptions* **Part 3 National Cinema** *Discussion & evaluation* **Part 4 Film Plots** *Identify genres & predict* **Part 5A/5B Movie Clichés** *Do's & Don'ts* **On Your Own**	***Main Discussion Areas*** *Good actors* *Types of films* *Typical films by country* *Movie stereotypes* ***Follow-on Activities*** *Create your own film* *Write a film review*
UNIT 10 **IRISH CULTURE** **& HISTORY** **Page 47**	**Warm Up / Quotes Section** **Part 1 Cultural Differences** *Read & match* **Part 2 History All Around Us** *Discuss & hypothesise* **On Your Own**	***Main Discussion Areas*** *Customs around the world* *Impact of history today* ***Follow-on Activities*** *Prepare cultural questions about your own country*
UNIT 11 **IRISH FESTIVALS** **& SOCIAL LIFE** **Page 51**	**Warm Up / Quotes Section** **Part 1 World Festivals** *Matching pictures & event* **Part 2A/2B Irish Festivals** *Explaining traditions* **Part 2C St. Patrick's Day** *Quiz. Hypothesise answers* **Part 3A/3B Drinks** *Match drink to occasion* **Part 4A/4B Irish Pub/Cheers** *Do's & Don'ts* **Part 5 Dinner Party** *Functional language* **On Your Own**	***Main Discussion Areas*** *How we celebrate festivals* *History of Irish festivals* *Drink culture & pub etiquette* *What to say at a dinner party* ***Follow-on Activities*** *Attend a festival in Ireland* *Have an international food night*
UNIT 12 **IRISH** **FOOTBALL -** **SAIPAN** **Page 55**	**Warm Up / Quotes Section** **Part 1 Preparation** *Rank importance* **Part 2 Main Characters** *Choosing adjectives* **Part 3 Arrival** *Read & evaluate* **Part 4 Meeting** *Read & evaluate* **Part 5 Country Divided** *Listen, match, answer* **Part 6/7 World Cup/After** *True or false quiz* **On Your Own**	***Main Discussion Areas*** *Evaluating a situation* *Evaluating characters* *What happens next* *Giving your opinion* ***Follow-on Activities*** *Watch documentary* *Read newspaper article* *Find out Irish people's opinions*

INTRODUCTION

THE IRISH CULTURE BOOK 2 - STUDENT BOOK includes a wide range of resources and activities designed to foster engagement and discussion on aspects of Irish culture. It can be used by any student with an interest in improving their English language skills and exploring areas of Irish culture.

THE IRISH CULTURE BOOK is most appropriate for language students of B1 level upwards although many activities will also be suitable for lower levels.

THE IRISH CULTURE BOOK is designed to give you, the student, opportunities to speak and think about topics that will be of interest about Ireland. The activities will help develop your conversation skills and improve your fluency through sharing ideas and observations. The conversations deepen critical thinking skills, helping to give the cultural awareness and speaking skills essential to be successful in a new culture and also for studying in college and university programs.

The material in THE IRISH CULTURE BOOK consists of twelve topic-based units on different areas of Irish culture, each filled with a variety of interesting and thought-provoking activities. The units all contain authentic texts. There are over three hundred and fifty questions, over one hundred quotations, including Irish proverbs and idioms; as well as questionnaires, matching and correcting exercises; reading, listening and vocabulary exercises; quizzes and creative problem-solving tasks. In many of the activities, students get to work together in pairs or small groups to reach a conclusion about a topic. A unique and important feature of the book is the inclusion of an 'On Your Own' section that calls on you to further investigate topics outside of the book, to initiate your own projects or to reflect on aspects of your own cultures in light of what has been discussed.

All the listening extracts used in THE IRISH CULTURE BOOK can be sourced online at **www.irishculturebook.com** and here can also be found further links and backup resources to each unit.

I hope you enjoy using this book.

IAN O'MALLEY

NOTES FOR STUDENTS

The joy of conversation and discussion in a language – moments of exchanging ideas, sharing experiences, collecting information, laughter and more…

Welcome to THE IRISH CULTURE BOOK.

The topics in the book are designed so that hopefully they are relevant to your own experiences of, and interest in, Irish culture. The exercises and discussions will give you a better understanding of Ireland and its people. You will have lots of opportunities to think about many areas of Irish culture, and as a language learner, lots of possibilities for improving your language at the same time.

If you are using the book by yourself, feel free to use it how you want. You don't have to do each exercise in the order they appear in the book. If you think an exercise is too difficult for you or you are more interested in another topic, you can jump forward to something else. You can always come back to the original exercise later.

You don't need to answer or think about every question. Read the questions, and the quotations and select the ones that you are most interested in thinking about. Don't just think about them directly. Ask yourself - do the questions remind you of any experience you've had yourself in Irish culture or do they make you think about anything in your own culture?

*On THE IRISH CULTURE BOOK website, **www.irishculturebook.com,** you can find links to lots more resources for each unit as well as all the listening files for the book.*

Specific guideline notes for each unit, as well as a range of background information and answer keys, are available in THE IRISH CULTURE BOOK - Teacher's Resource Book.

And finally, the idea of the book is that we begin to think about and discuss, in English, what makes our cultures what they are. So don't be afraid to disagree with what you read in the book. Your ideas on Irish culture may be equally as valid as any of the observations offered in the book.

STRUCTURE OF A UNIT

Most units in the book follow the general structure outlined below.

WARM-UP Section

The questions in the WARM-UP section are intended as an initial introduction to the unit topic, focusing on the learner's personal experience and opinions, and also finding out how much, if anything, is known about the topic about to be discussed. For teachers, feel free to skip some or all of the questions or ask your own questions if you feel they are more appropriate for your particular class.

QUOTATIONS Section

The quotations present a wide range of ideas, viewpoints and perspectives. Quotations can be particularly appealing to language learners of all levels because they give an immediate, easy access into a piece of wisdom or life-view expressed in another language. Quotations are excellent for provoking debate and give the discussions a deeper perspective. There are many ways to use this section.

- For all users, feel free to read through all the quotations or focus on just a couple.
- Think about if there is any quotation you disagree with and why, or which quotation most reflects your own view.
- With proverbs, sayings or idioms, try to think if you have any similar or equivalent sayings in your own culture.
- As a teacher, you could ask students to read through the quotations themselves and to choose their favourite one and report back to the class.
- As a teacher of a multicultural class, you could ask students to translate any proverb, saying or idiom from their own language and share it with the class.

PARTS 1 - 5

Most units are divided into three to five parts. These parts are the main body of each unit and include quizzes, problem-solving activities, questions, short readings, listenings, matching exercises and more.

- For each unit, consult the instructions and supporting materials in the Supplementary Notes.
- It is not necessary to do every part of a unit depending on time constraints or interest or, for teachers, the language proficiency of your students
- Also, feel free to change the order in which you do these parts as you wish.

ON YOUR OWN Section

This section encourages you to think outside of the book or classroom. It may involve:

- Project or written work.
- Asking questions of Irish people about their ideas of the topic of the unit and reporting back.
- Reflection on the users' own cultures in comparison/contrast to Irish culture and reporting back.
- Further reflection on the users' own opinions and ideas on the topics raised in the unit.

ACKNOWLEDGEMENTS

I would like to thank all the people who supported and assisted in making this book possible.

Thank you to all the students of DCI who helped test and refine materials and provided a lot of fun while doing it - to Anna from Ukraine, Damien from France, Tania and Sofia from Uruguay, Linan from China, Yeojae from South Korea, Luisina, Roberto and Pablo from Argentina, Patricia, Lilian and Elisa from Brazil, Norman from Singapore, Karina and Svetlana from Russia and many others.

A big thank you to the models Nicoletta Giusti, Ruth Wall and Federico Black and for the voice work of Jimena, Svetlana, Salah and others.

Thank you to the talented teachers and colleagues for their advice - to Anthony, Niall, Ana, Aonghus, Felicity, Mark, Daniel and others.

A huge thank you to those who suggested amendments or supported in different ways - to Shaun O'Malley, to Jim and Eimear and the Gormans, Mark Rae, Dervla O'Malley, Vera O'Malley, Fiona McGinty, Niamh Kelly and Ania Tomaszewska.

It has not always been possible to identify the sources of all the material used in the book and in such cases the publisher and author would welcome information from the copyright owners.

A special mention for two great teachers I've learned so much from - my uncle Tom and my aunt Ellen - and also for my friend Andrew who always inspired me to gaze further and think bigger.

Thanks and love to all my family who helped and supported at different points - to all the rest of the O'Malleys, Roma, Lisa, Shane, Emer and Niall; to Keelan and Evan and all the Finns; to Leah, Cameron, Cian and all the Raes.

COMMENTS AND FEEDBACK

Your feedback is extremely welcome.
Please get in contact and let us know your opinions on the book.

E-mail:

ian@irishculturebook.com

Web-page:

www.irishculturebook.com

WARM UP

1. What do you know about Ireland - for example its history, geography, language, food, religion, legends or politics?
2. Do you know of any famous Irish people?
3. What are your impressions of Irish people in general?

PART 1 AROUND THE WORLD

1. How much do you know? Match each country with a fact in the grid below and then also with a picture.

A. Canada B. Ireland C. Brazil D. New Zealand E. Russia F. China G. Greece H. Egypt I. France

FACT	COUNTRY	PICTURE
First Olympics were held here in 776 BC		
Famous for *Samba* dancing		
First country in the world to ban smoking in pubs and workplaces		
This country has the longest coastline and the most lakes in the world		
Where the first photograph was taken		
Where gunpowder was invented		
Contains the longest river in the world		
First man in space was from here		
Bungee jumping was invented here		

2. Is your country included here? What (other) pictures and facts would you use to represent your country?
3. What other facts/pictures could you use for Ireland?

Hmm... Life is just too short not to be Irish.

PART 2 TWENTY QUESTIONS ABOUT IRELAND
WHAT DO YOU KNOW ABOUT IRELAND? TEST YOUR KNOWLEDGE BELOW.

1. What symbol is on the front of all Irish Euro coins?

2. What sea is off Ireland's east coast? **A.** *Grey Sea* **B.** *Green Sea* **C.** *Irish Sea* **D.** *English Sea*

3. Name one of Ireland's airline companies. *(Bonus point - name one other Irish company)*

4. Name a famous Irish actor. *(Bonus point - name an Irish film)*

5. What colour do the Irish football team play in? *(Bonus point - what is the away shirt colour?)*

6. Give examples of two traditional Irish names. *(Bonus point - 2 x men's and 2 x women's names)*

7. Name three Irish cities.

8. Is Ireland **A.** *the 10th* **B.** *the 20th* **C.** *the 30th* biggest island in the world?

9. The festival of Halloween originated in Ireland. On what date is it each year?

PART 2 TWENTY QUESTIONS ABOUT IRELAND *contd.*

10. Can you name two groups of people that Ireland has been invaded by during its history?

11. What atmospheric 'effect', which heats the earth and is a cause of climate change, did Irish scientist John Tyndall discover? **A.** *Sauna Effect* **B.** *Greenhouse Effect* **C.** *Sunbed Effect*

12. What are the main ingredients of Irish Stew?

13. Name one of Ireland's national sports. *(Bonus point - name a famous Irish sportsperson)*

14. What do *Mac* or *O'* mean in Irish surnames? *(Bonus point - give an example of each surname)*

15. What drink did writer James Joyce call *'the wine of the Irish'*?

16. Name two traditional Irish musical instruments.

17. What famous building in the USA did Irish architect James Hoban design?

18. What is the Internet address for Ireland?

TYNDALL   JOYCE   HOBAN

PART 2 TWENTY QUESTIONS ABOUT IRELAND *contd.*

19. What is the most common eye colour in Ireland?

20. Which of these was <u>not</u> invented in Ireland? **A.** *The submarine* **B.** *St. Patrick's Day parades* **C.** *The flavoured potato crisp* **D.** *Soda water* **E.** *Colour photography*

BONUS QUESTION 1

Match the four Irish provinces with the numbers on the map of Ireland.

PROVINCE	NUMBER ON MAP
MUNSTER	
LEINSTER	
CONNACHT	
ULSTER	

BONUS QUESTION 2

Match the six pictures of famous Irish people with their names and with the interesting facts about them.

NAME			
i.	Conor McGregor	iv.	Saoirse Ronan
ii.	Pierce Brosnan	v.	Katie Taylor
iii.	Wellington	vi.	Dracula

INTERESTING FACT	
A.	Olympic gold boxing champion
B.	Defeated Napoleon's army at Waterloo
C.	He has no mirrors in his house
D.	Actor who played James Bond
E.	Nominated for two Oscars
F.	Voted 'Ireland's Most Stylish Person'

PICTURE	NAME	FACT
1		
2		
3		
4		
5		
6		

ON YOUR OWN

1. Pick one question which you found interesting. Look up more information about this area of Irish culture.
2. CREATE YOUR OWN QUIZ: Make a list of general knowledge questions about your country. Ask them to your class.

WARM UP

1. Which sports do you like to play or watch?
2. Who is your favourite sportsperson? Why?
3. What is the most popular sport in your country?
4. What was your country's 'greatest sporting moment'?
5. What do you know about Irish sports?

PART 1 'FASTER, HIGHER, STRONGER'

1. TRIVIA QUESTION: What colour are the five Olympic rings?
2. Can you match the Olympic sports with the symbols below?

OLYMPIC SPORT	SYMBOL	OLYMPIC SPORT	SYMBOL
Badminton		Ice Hockey	
Kayaking		Swimming	
Judo		Diving	
Volleyball		Athletics	
Weightlifting		Archery	
Handball		Table Tennis	
Boxing		Cycling	
Gymnastics		Skiing	

3. Which of the sports above would you most like to try? Why?
4. Design symbols to represent some sports in the box below (or other sports). Get other students to guess the sport.

> *Football – basketball – baseball – tennis – long jump*
> *hockey – rugby – high jump – snowboarding – golf*

5. In which Olympic sports is your country most successful?
6. Which Olympic sports do you think Ireland is strongest in?
7. What factors influence why countries are good at specific sports? *(Environment, weather, tradition, physique etc.)*

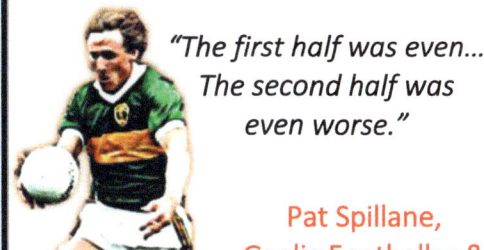

"The first half was even... The second half was even worse."

Pat Spillane,
Gaelic Footballer &
TV Commentator

PART 2A GAELIC GAMES

1. TRUE OR FALSE QUIZ: Ireland's national sports are Gaelic football, hurling, camogie and handball. They are run by the Gaelic Athletic Association (GAA). **Decide if the facts below are TRUE or FALSE.**

GAA FACTS	T/F
Gaelic footballers earn a lot of money for playing	
Hurling has been played in Ireland for about 100 years	
Many camogie players wear skorts (skirt/shorts)	
Ireland play Gaelic football internationals against Australia	
The GAA was important in the fight for independence from Britain	
The GAA stadium Croke Park is the 3rd biggest in Europe	
Hurling was inspired by Canada's national sport ice hockey	
ESPN's 'Top Ten World Sporting Events To See Live' - The All-Ireland Final is listed third, one place behind the football World Cup final	

2. What is the national sport in your country? Make TRUE/FALSE Facts about it and test your class.
3. **GAELIC GAMES: HOW TO PLAY** Watch some video of Gaelic football and hurling (See ONLINE SECTION). What do you think of the two sports? Match the Rules in the box to the correct Sport.

> **A.** Games last seventy minutes **B.** Like a mix of rugby & soccer **C.** You hit the ball with a stick
> **D.** Teams of fifteen players **E.** Ball over the bar = one point / Ball into the net = a goal or three points
> **F.** Like hockey but you can pick the ball up into your hands **G.** You can't throw the ball
> **H.** Kick or punch the ball to pass & to score **I.** As you run, balance the ball on the stick
> **J.** As you run, bounce the ball or drop it onto your foot

Point

Goal

GAELIC FOOTBALL		HURLING		BOTH	

4. Write out the rules for a sport - the other students must guess which sport it is.
5. If you have access to a ball/hurl/sliothar, practice some of the Gaelic games skills above for yourself.

CULTURAL IMPORTANCE OF GAELIC GAMES

In 1884, a group of nationalistic Irishmen founded the GAA to bring structure to traditional Irish sports and to promote Irish cultural identity. Michael Cusack, 'Father of the GAA', said, 'A race of people is dependant on its sports for the development of a national spirit.'

a. Why do you think these men were worried about the decline of Irish culture and sports at this time (1880s)? Do you agree with Cusack's quote?
b. What does 'cultural nationalism' mean? Can you give an example from your country?

Today there are over 2,500 GAA clubs in Ireland and many others among emigrant communities all around the world. Gaelic games are played in the thirty counties of the island, both north and south. The All-Ireland finals are held each year in September in Croke Park, Dublin, which holds over 82,000 people. The players are all unpaid amateurs who represent their local communities.

c. Do you think GAA players should get paid? Why/why not?
d. Find out which counties are the most successful in hurling, Gaelic football and camogie. Choose a team to support in the All Irelands - learn about their history, team colours and songs, best players etc.

PART 2B THE LEGEND OF HURLING

Read the story of how the ancient Irish hero Cú Chulainn got his name...

Long ago, an important man called Culann organised a big party. He invited King Conor and many other people including Setanta, a young boy who worked for the King. Culann put his best guard dog outside the entrance to protect his castle during the party. However, Setanta was playing a game of hurling and arrived late. He was walking along bouncing the sliotar (ball) on his hurley. The huge dog was waiting and attacked Setanta. Terrified, Setanta used all his strength to hit the sliotar with his hurley. It went straight into the hound's throat and killed it. Later, Culann was happy Setanta was safe but sad his dog had died. Setanta said that he would guard Culann's castle until he got another dog. The Irish word for a dog or hound is Cú (Coo). Setanta became known as Cú Chulainn – 'The Hound of Culann.'

1. Can you research or invent a legend for how another sport began?

PART 3A IRISH SPORTING GREATS

1. Can you match the pictures with the famous Irish sportspeople and with their achievements?

SPORTSPERSON
1. Sean Kelly – *Cycling*
2. Henry Shefflin – *Hurling*
3. Eddie Irvine – *Formula 1*
4. Robbie Keane – *Football*
5. Sonia O'Sullivan – *Athletics*
6. AP McCoy – *Horse Racing*
7. Brian O'Driscoll – *Rugby*
8. Katie Taylor – *Boxing*
9. Padraig Harrington – *Golf*

ACHIEVEMENT
A. Scored forty-six tries for Ireland
B. Won three 'Majors'
C. 5000 metre Olympic silver medallist
D. All Ireland Champion ten times
E. Won four Grand Prix
F. Won Tour of Spain
G. Olympic lightweight champion
H. Scored sixty-eight goals for Ireland
I. 'Jockey of Year' twenty times

PICTURE	i	ii	iii	iv	v	vi	vii	viii	ix
SPORTSPERSON									
ACHIEVEMENT									

2. Which achievement do you think is the most impressive? Find out more about one of the sports stars and report back to the class. Do you know any other Irish sportspeople?
3. What is your personal 'greatest' sporting achievement? (It can be big or small!)

PART 3B WHO IS YOUR COUNTRY'S GREATEST?

1. The sports stars below are some of the greatest, most loved athletes of their countries. Match each to their country.

1 Usain Bolt Athletics	Romania
2 Steffi Graf Tennis	Philippines
3 Steve Redgrave Rowing	Austria
4 Michael Jordan Basketball	Jamaica
5 Imran Khan Cricket	England
6 Wayne Gretzky Ice Hockey	Pakistan
7 Manny Pacquiao Boxing	USA
8 Maradona Football	Germany
9 Nadia Comaneci Gymnastics	Canada
10 Hermann Maier Skiing	Argentina

2. Does the sport help you to match some of the sportspeople to their country? How?
3. What factors are important in making an athlete popular? Is 'character' important or only the sporting achievements?
4. If your country is included above, do you agree with the athlete chosen? If not, who do you think should represent your country as 'greatest' or 'most loved' sportsperson? Give reasons for your choice.

PART 4 AN IRISH SPORTING MOMENT

SPORTING RIVALS: *1. Who is your country's biggest sporting rival? Why? Is it for sporting reasons/political/historical reasons etc?*

2.   Who do you think is the team Ireland always wants to defeat in sport? Why do you think this ... you know about Ireland's history?)

BLOODY SUNDAY: On the morning of November 21st, 1920, during the War of Independence, fourteen British military officers were killed by Irish secret agents. Later that day, Tipperary played Dublin in Gaelic football at Croke Park. During the game, British soldiers attacked fans in the stadium, killing fourteen.

3.   Why do you think the British army chose to attack people at a Gaelic football match?

THE STADIUM: In 2007, the rugby stadium in Dublin was being rebuilt and the rugby association asked to borrow Croke Park for some international matches in the Six Nations. This caused huge debate and controversy.

4.   Croke Park was always the stadium for Gaelic games but why do you think playing the 'foreign' sport of rugby there was so controversial? (American football had been played there before with no problem.)

5.   What arguments do you think there were 'for' and 'against' allowing rugby to be played in Croke Park?

THE SPORT: *6. Have you ever watched a rugby match? Can you understand/explain the basic rules?*

7.   Do you know what teams play in the rugby Six Nations Championship?

NATIONAL ANTHEMS: The GAA finally agreed to allow rugby to be played in Croke Park. In Feb 2007, the rugby world champions, England, arrived at Croke Park. There was a lot of tension before the match.

8.   Why do you think people were so worried before the start of the match about the anthems?

9.   Eddie O'Sullivan, Ireland Coach - 'I had great confidence the Irish fans would do the right thing during the anthems.' What do you think the 'right thing' to do was? What would you do as a fan?

THE MATCH: Girvan Dempsey, player - *'It was the most emotional game I've ever been involved in.'*

10.   Do you think the extra emotion would help the Irish team or not?

Shane Horgan, player - *'The last thing we wanted was to embarrass ourselves vs. England in Croke Park.'*

11.   Some of the players described losing to England in Croke Park as 'unthinkable'. What does this mean?

THE RESULT: *12. Who do you think won? Look online and find out. (See ONLINE SECTION).*

YOUR COUNTRY: *13. Tell your class about an important sporting moment in your country. Why was it so significant? Did people who normally had no interest in sport become involved in it etc?*

ON YOUR OWN

1.   Invent a sport. Or design a new sports stadium. Or design a sports jersey.

2.   Create the perfect sportsperson. What physical and mental characteristics should he/she have? Give reasons.

3.   Ask an Irish person about their favourite sports star/team/sport. Report back.

4.   Go watch a live Gaelic football, hurling or camogie game. Or some other live sports event in Ireland.

5.   Try playing Gaelic football, hurling or camogie yourself!

WARM UP

1. What characteristics do you value most in a friend?
2. What do you think is a good age to get married? (Why?)
3. Finish these sentences: *I think I am……………………………*
   Other people say I am……………………………
4. What is your favourite song/animal? Write three adjectives to describe each. *(Ask your teacher for an explanation.)*

PART 1A NATIONAL CHARACTER

1. Can you give one example of a stereotype of men and women? Do you think this stereotype is true or false?
2. Can you give an example of a national stereotype? Is it true? (Or is generalising about whole nations unhelpful?)
3. Cultures often have their own stereotypes of themselves. Can you think of any for your country? Match each country below with its self-stereotype and the descriptions.

Ireland - Italy - England - USA - Japan - India - Germany

SELF-STEREOTYPE	**A.** 'Can do attitude' **B.** 'Having the craic' **C.** 'Efficiency' **D.** 'Saving face' **E.** 'Karma' **F.** 'La Bella figura'

DESCRIPTION
1. Beauty, style and public image are very important to us
2. We don't admit mistakes or publicly disagree with superiors
3. We're spiritual. We accept the good and bad that life brings
4. We laugh at ourselves and try to find fun in any situation
5. We're well-organised. We follow the rules & like structure
6. We believe in positivity. Work hard and you'll achieve success

COUNTRY	Ire	It	USA	Jap	Ind	Ger
SELF-STEREOTYPE						
DESCRIPTION						

4. Is your country included? Do you agree with the description? If not, write your own national character description.
5. Are you 'typical' of someone from your country?
6. What would you think of as a 'typical' Irish person?

PART 1B I'D LIKE TO GET TO KNOW

1. Do you like meeting new people? Are you good at it?
2. *Close your eyes. Imagine someone you'd really like to meet or know better. When ready, complete the sentences below.*

I'D LIKE TO GET TO KNOW...

A...
Who has...
Who wears…
Whose most important possession is…
Whose passion…
And who…
If I want…

3. What are good ways to meet people in a new country?
4. In general, who do you think are easier to get to know - people from your country or Irish people? Why?

QUOTES

Which is your favourite quote? Why?

"There are no strangers here, only friends you haven't yet met." – **WB Yeats**

"Meeting people of other nations is the best cure for prejudice & narrow-mindedness." – **Mark Twain**

"Stereotypes lose power the moment we talk to an individual." – **Ed Koch**

"People would never fall in love if they hadn't heard about the idea of love."
– **François de La Rochefoucauld**

"The best feeling is knowing you are special to someone." – **Jade Fennell**

"Never love anyone who treats you like you're ordinary." – **Oscar Wilde**

"Every time you find humour in a difficult situation, you win." – **Snoopy**

"A sense of humour is common sense moving at a different speed, it's common sense dancing." – **William James**

"I'm not funny. I just tell people the truth & they say haha you're funny" – **Jon Hart**

"Laughter on your lips is a good sign you understand life." – **Hugh Sidey**

"If you don't love me, I won't be loved. If I don't love you, I won't love."
– **Samuel Beckett**

"To be Irish is to know the world will break your heart." – **Virginia Henley**

"The only cure for love is marriage."
– **Irish Proverb**

Share your genuine feelings about the quotes… join the discussion. Can you share any similar quotes from your own culture?

So, we've grown old together. What now?

Bungee jumping?

UNIT 3 IRISH CHARACTER & RELATIONSHIPS

PART 2A WHAT DO YOU LOOK FOR IN A PARTNER?

1. Rank the qualities below (1-10) in order of importance for you in a boyfriend/girlfriend.

	is patient & kind		is physically attractive
	has a good sense of humour		has similar interests
	has a good family background		has a good career
	gets on well with your family/friends		is intelligent
	can express his/her feelings		is from the same culture as you

2. In pairs, compare your answers. Can you agree on a Top 5 together? Give reasons for your choices.
3. Are there universal qualities that we all search for in a romantic relationship?
4. Do these three factors - *Stage of life / Gender / Culture* - have a big impact on what we want?

PART 2B ROMANCE AROUND THE WORLD

1. Can you match the five countries to their romantic style?

A. IRELAND **B.** SWEDEN **C.** FRANCE **D.** KOREA **E.** ARGENTINA	
	Elegance & style. Good food & wine. Talk deeply about love & romance
	Passionate, hot-blooded & sensual as expressed in their dance as well as their relationships
	Equality. Non-traditional gender roles - independent women & men who share the housework
	Fun & informal. Easy-going, few melodramas, lots of conversation & let's see what happens
	Polite & respectful. Traditional roles. Family has big influence. Cute 'couples t-shirts/hats'

2. Which romantic style would attract you most? Why? What do you think of the Irish approach?
3. Is/Should your country be on the list? Are you romantic? What other nations do you think are romantic?

PART 2C DATING

1. In your country, is dating usually something serious or is it often just for fun?
2. Describe a typical first date in your country. Who invites who? Who pays? Etc.
3. When was the last time you were on a date? Did it go well?
4. TASK 1: Imagine two people from different cultures go out on a first date. Make a list of at least three cross-cultural difficulties they might face. Can you also list some advantages in dating someone from another culture? In pairs/small groups, write the conversation the couple might have.
5. TASK 2: Research how Irish people date. Have you experienced dating in Ireland? How different is it from your country? What cross-cultural challenges do you think you might face being in a relationship with an Irish person?
6. TASK 3: Do people in your country use online dating? Has this changed how people date? Invent your own imaginary dating profile. Be creative. Exchange profiles with other students and write messages introducing yourselves.

PART 2D 'WHERE DO I STAND IN THIS RELATIONSHIP?'

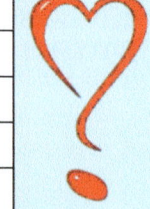

1. In groups, can you put the stages of a relationship in the correct order (1-10)? (Can you agree on a 'correct' order?)

	To date / see someone	To flirt with
	To get married	To fancy / have a crush on someone
	To get engaged	To move in together
	To go out with	To meet the parents
	To go on a date	To get off with (Br) / Make out with (Am) / Shift or Snog (Ire)

2. Every relationship is different but how long on average would the stages above take in your country? (Eg. Meet the parents after six months together?) Is there pressure to be married by a certain age in your country?
3. Are the relationship stages different in your country? For example, do you have arranged marriages? Etc.
4. In Ireland, things have changed a lot. Couples marry later. They often live together before getting married. Divorce was made legal in 1996, same-sex marriage became legal in 2015. Is this similar to/different from your country?
5. If you're in a relationship, think about the stages you went through. (How did you get together? Etc.) Share with the class if you like. Are your experiences similar to or very different from the others in the class?

PART 3A 'A FUNNY THING HAPPENED ON THE WAY TO LOVE'

1. How high did you rank 'sense of humour' in PART 2A? Someone who makes us laugh seems to have universal appeal around the world. ***Match the paragraph titles with the theories below explaining why.***

1. SHOWS ATTRACTIVE QUALITIES	2. REVEALS INTEREST	3. CREATES TOGETHERNESS	

A.	*A man joking and woman laughing (or not) is a way for him to judge if she's attracted to him and for her to show attraction. This romance 'script' is generations old.*
B.	*A shared laugh brings people together. It shows values or life-views in common. It makes us feel good together and is a pathway to a longer-lasting relationship.*
C.	*Humour is about timing - saying something at the right time to the right people. It suggests emotional and social intelligence and a likeable personality.*

2. Which do you agree with most? Do you agree humour plays a different role in flirting for men/women?
3. 'Humour is best used in moderation on a first date.' Why? Have you experienced when 'a joke goes wrong'?

PART 3B WHAT TYPE OF HUMOUR ARE YOU?

1. Who is your funniest friend? What makes them so funny?
2. What is your favourite comedy film, TV show or comedian? What do you not find funny?
3. Can you match the six humour types to the descriptions below? *(Look up any words you don't know.)*

1. LAUGH-AT-LIFE 2. WITTY 3. ANECDOTAL 4. IRONIC 5. SELF-DEPRECATING 6. DEADPAN

	Telling funny or humorous stories (they can be true or partly true)
	The intended meaning is opposite to the actual words said
	Making fun of yourself
	Looking for the humour in a situation (even a bad one) & laughing
	Saying a funny line without smiling while everyone else is laughing
	Your jokes show intelligence & an ability to play with language

4. Which humour do you like most? Which is most common in your culture?
5. TASK: Find video of something that makes you laugh. Show it to the class. Is it one of the humour types above? Do the other students find it funny?

PART 3C IRISH SENSE OF HUMOUR

1. Is it difficult to understand humour in another culture? Why? Have you ever experienced 'not getting the joke'?
2. Understanding the Irish sense of humour is important in getting to know the people. Some key characteristics are explained below that might help you understand better. Can you link each box to a type of humour in 3B above?

A. Irish people don't take themselves too seriously. They make jokes about themselves and also like others who can laugh at themselves too so there's a lot of slagging. Often the more Irish insult you, the more they like you.	D. Sit in a pub or listen to Irish people talk about their weekends on a Monday in work. Irish love telling stories to make each other laugh. The ability to tell funny stories is valued. People listen and appreciate.
B. Irish people will say something with a smile and a look in their eyes. Are they being serious? Did they mean that statement or was that sarcasm?	E. An Irish person will say something with a straight face and no indication that he/she is making a joke. It only hits you a couple of seconds later.
C. Irish joke all the time – in the saddest situation like a funeral (to celebrate the person's life with laughter) or the most serious business work meeting. Humour is present everywhere – making fun of the good and bad in life.	F. Irish people can be eloquent speakers and really inventive and clever in how they use language for comic effect. Irish also use a lot of 'bad language'. It is not in an aggressive way, just for comic emphasis.

3. Have you experienced any of these aspects of Irish humour?
4. A – What does 'slagging' mean? Do you have friendships where you slag each other a lot?
5. C – Would it happen in your culture that people joke in a business meeting? Or even at a funeral?
6. F – *'English is a wall between us and our true Irish character. Bad language is a hammer.'* – Comedian, Tommy Tiernan. What does he mean? Who uses bad language in your country? In what contexts?
7. TASK: Tell a joke to your friends. Your task is to make them laugh.

PART 4A 'TÁ MÉ I NGRÁ LEAT'

1. How do you say *'I love you'* in your language? Try saying it in Irish above. How many of the languages on the right do you know?
2. From *'I like you'* to *'I love you'* is a big jump in any relationship. What phrases do you use in your language? Can you rank the love statements in English below 1-8 from the least to most serious - from like to love?

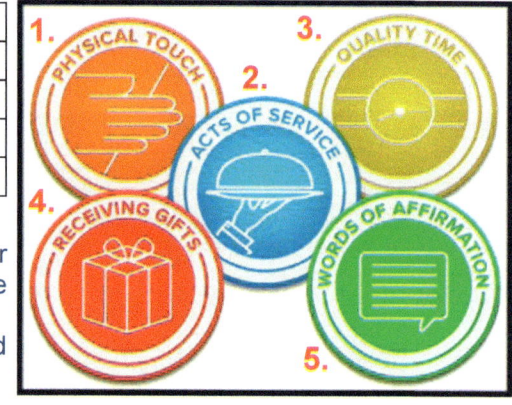

	I've feelings for you		I kind of like you
	I'm in love with you		I'm mad/crazy about you
	I care about you		I have a thing for you
	I'm falling for you		I really really really like you

3. Which terms of affection below do you like most? Can you translate any ones from your language?

My partner - My lover - My other half	*Sweetie - Darling - Baby - Love - Pet - Dear - Sugar - Honey*

4. Love isn't always easy... Have you said/heard any of the expressions below? Which is the worst to hear?

> *I want to take this slow - I think we should take a break - It's not you, it's me*
> *It's just bad timing - I love you but I'm not in love with you - There are plenty more fish in the sea*

PART 4B THE FIVE LOVE LANGUAGES

1. Words are not the only way to express our feelings for somebody. Apparently, there are five basic ways in which we all express love. Match the descriptions below to the love languages on the right.

A symbol of your affection makes him/her feel loved	
Your undivided attention is worth more than any present	
Doing housework or helping out is saying you love him/her	
Compliments and praise mean a lot. Hard words hurt	
An embrace or sitting close makes him/her feel loved	

2. Which love language do you think is strongest for you?
3. Are you in a relationship? Which language do you think is strongest for your partner? Is it different from yours? Why do you think this might be important?
4. Which way of expressing affection do you think is strongest or most used in general in your culture? What about in Ireland?

PART 5 FORBIDDEN LOVE

1. Why might a couple not be able to be together in your culture now or in the past? What about in Ireland?
2. Read the story below about 'Forbidden Love' and answer the questions.

It was a cold, dark night. The two of them were alone together in the house. The storm had come quickly and each time the thunder boomed, he watched her jump. She looked across the room and admired his strong appearance. She wanted, more than anything, that he would take her in his arms and protect her. Suddenly, with a pop, the power went out. She screamed. He rushed to the sofa where she was sitting, afraid. He didn't hesitate to pull her into his arms. He knew this was a forbidden union and expected her to pull back. He was surprised when she didn't resist but instead held him tightly. The storm continued as their feelings for each other grew. There came a moment when each knew that they had to be together. They knew it was wrong. Their families would never understand. They were so focused on their passion for each other that they didn't hear the door opening... just the quiet click of a camera...

3. Who are the two people and why is it a 'forbidden union'? Think of different possibilities.
4. *'Just the quiet click of a camera...'* Who do you think is taking the photograph?
5. Vote on the most likely situation. *To see the photograph, ask your teacher or check the ONLINE SECTION.*

ON YOUR OWN

1. Think of somebody important in your life. Send them a message in English to say how much you care about them.
2. Watch an Irish TV comedy series or go see an Irish stand-up comedian live. Can you 'get' the jokes?
3. An English-speaking boy/girlfriend is great for improving your English. Go find one! Just joking... (Or are we?)

WARM UP

1. What thing in your life could you not live without? Why?
2. Can you think of a bad invention you'd like to <u>un</u>-invent?
3. NEW USES: We normally use a clothes hanger to hang clothes. In pairs, use your imagination and try to think of four or five other possible uses. (*Eg. you could use it as TV antennae etc.*)

PART 1 TEN WORLD INVENTIONS

1. Match the inventions with When/Where each was invented.

	1 Velcro	2 Cinema	3 Lego
	4 Flushing Toilet	5 Coffee	6 Paper
	7 Car	8 Glasses	
	9 Internet	10 Zero	

WHEN/WHERE	
	2nd C. China
	7th C. India
	10th C. Ethiopia
	1280 Italy
	1596 UK
	1886 Germany
	1890s France
	1948 Switzerland
	1958 Denmark
	1969 USA

2. In pairs, rank the inventions above in order of importance.
3. Choose a Top Three (not including the inventions above) for the most useful human inventions ever and the Top Three most useful inventions in your lifetime. Give reasons.

TOP 3 IN HISTORY	TOP 3 IN YOUR LIFETIME

4. If you time-travelled back three hundred years, what inventions could you actually make to improve people's lives back then?
5. What not-yet-invented thing do you think the world really needs?

"How interesting! A new scientific report claims that 50% of people find scientific reports boring."

UNIT 4 SCIENCE, INNOVATION & BUSINESS

PART 2A TEN IRISH INVENTIONS

1. Match the Irish inventions to the descriptions below and to the timeline of when each was invented.

| 1 Ejector Seat | 2 Tank | 3 Rubber-soled shoes | 4 WiFi | 5 Chocolate Milk |
| 6 Tattoo Machine | 7 Heart Defibrillator | 8 Syringe | 9 Football Penalty | 10 Tractor |

DESCRIPTION	PICTURE
A. Changed the face of war	
B. It hurts, then helps	
C. Causes controversy	
D. More comfortable	
E. A life-saver	
F. Keeping children happy	
G. Changed the face of farming	
H. Making people cool	
I. Staying connected	
J. A quick escape	

TIMELINE		
Which invention was invented first? *(1680)*		
Which was invented last? *(1996)*		
Match *'ejector seat'*, *'tractor'* & *'tank'* to the dates		
1911	*1926*	*1946*
Which piece of medical equipment came first - the *defibrillator* or the *syringe?*		
(1844)		*(1965)*
Which three things were invented in the 1890s?		

2. Which one surprises you most that it was invented in Ireland? Find out more about how it was invented.
3. What are your country's most famous inventions? If you don't know any, research and share back.

PART 2B GULLIVER'S TRAVELS – ADAPT & SURVIVE

1. **GULLIVER'S TRAVELS** was written by Irish writer, **Jonathan Swift** in 1726. What do you know about the story? For example, what is special about the island of **Lilliput**, the first place that Gulliver visits?

2. After Lilliput, Gulliver travels to **Brobdingnag**, a land of giants where everything is twenty times bigger than normal. **TASK 1: (10 Mins)** Divide into teams. Imagine you are Gulliver and you're ready to leave Brobdingnag. Before getting in your boat, the giants want to give you some things to remember them by. (See box.) Everything is big, so you can only fit six things in your boat. You don't know where you will go, so choose your six things carefully!

Box of matches – Cork – Handkerchief – Biscuit – Nail scissors – Gold coin – Map – Comb Toothbrush – Pencil – Small mirror – Shoelace – Notebook – Key – Watch – Necklace Bar of Soap – Chewing gum – Credit card – Bottle of perfume – Pen – Ring

3. After one week in your boat, you meet a huge storm. Your boat is destroyed and you are washed up on a desert island with just the six objects you brought. The island is normal sized with trees, plants and plenty of water. It is very hot during the day, cold at night and has lots of dangerous animals.
TASK 2: (10 Mins) Using the six objects and what is on the island, you must find a way to:

1. Stay cool during the day	2. Stay warm at night
3. Find food	4. Protect yourself from the dangerous animals

4. **TASK 3:** Present your team's ideas to the whole class. Vote on whose ideas are best and who is most likely to survive.

UNIT 4 SCIENCE, INNOVATION & BUSINESS

PART 3A IRISH SCIENCE QUIZ

A.   Do you like science? Why/why not? In pairs/small groups, test your scientific knowledge.

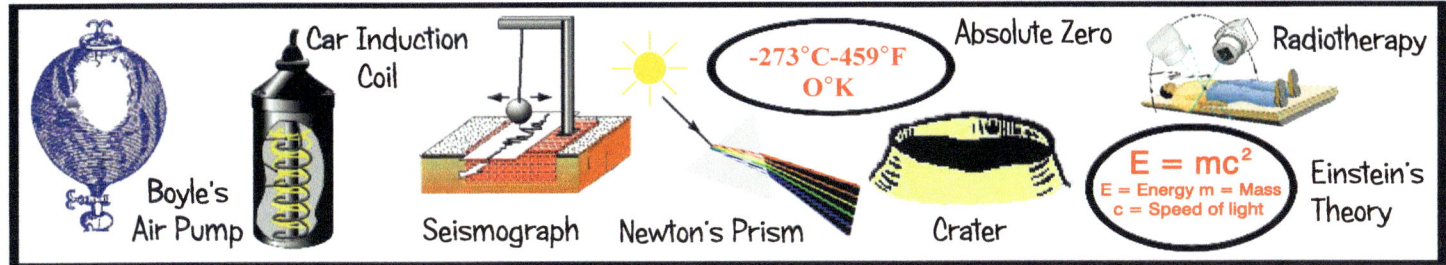

IRISH SCIENCE QUIZ: FAMOUS IRISH SCIENTISTS

1. **Robert Boyle** (1627-1691) has been called the 'Father of Modern Chemistry'. With his 'air pump' experiments, which three of the four things below did he prove air was necessary for?

A. To make fire	**B.** For breathing	**C.** For sound to travel	**D.** To fly a kite

2. **Nicholas Callan** invented the induction coil in 1836. What important function does it have in your car?

A. To start the engine	**B.** For turning left	**C.** To operate the radio	**D.** To stop

3. 'Seismology' was developed by **Robert Mallet** in 1851. What natural phenomenon does it study?

A. Hurricanes	**B.** Volcanoes	**C.** Earthquakes	**D.** Thunder & lightning

4. Building on Newton's prism experiment, what did **John Tyndall** (1820-1893) discover about the sky?

A. Why it's blue	**B.** Why it rains in Ireland	**C.** How birds fly	**D.** Where clouds come from

5. **William Thomson** developed the Kelvin scale, based around the principle of Absolute Zero (- 273°C), in 1848. If freezing point is '0°Celsius / 32°Fahrenheit / 273 Kelvin', what is boiling point in each scale?

Celsius:	*Fahrenheit:*	*Kelvin:*

6. The 'electron' was first calculated and described by **George Johnstone Stoney** (1826-1911). In the diagram, which part of an atom (A, B or C) is an electron?

7. What are the other two parts of an atom called?

i. Neutron & Megatron	**ii.** Proton & Galvatron
iii. Decepticon & Proton	**iv.** Proton & Neutron

8. **Agnes Clerke** (1842-1907) was an astronomical writer. She had a crater beside the 'Sea of Serenity' named after her. Where is the Sea of Serenity?

9. **John Joly** developed 'radiotherapy' in the 1910s. What is its main medical use today?

A. Takes x-rays of bones	**B.** Kills cancer cells	**C.** Helps eating problems	**D.** Good for headaches

10. **Ernest Walton** won the Nobel Prize for splitting the atom in 1932 (so demonstrating Einstein's $E=mc^2$ theory). Can you think of one positive and one negative consequence of this breakthrough?

POSITIVE:	*NEGATIVE:*

B.   Do you know your country's most famous scientists and what they achieved? If not, look them up.
C.   In groups, make a list of what you think are the three most important scientific breakthroughs in history.
D.   Can you think of any general knowledge science quiz questions to ask the other groups?
E.   For bonus points, can you explain 'Absolute Zero' or even '$E = mc^2$' to the rest of the class?

PART 3B THE IRISH ALSO INVENTED WIND

1. *'The wind was a 3 on the Beaufort scale.'* How we measure wind was developed by Irishman Francis Beaufort. Can you match the example Beaufort scale categories on the left with the wind effects we experience in the box?

BEAUFORT CATEGORIES	EFFECTS
0 Calm *(Less than 1 kmph)*	
2 Light breeze *(6-11 kmph)*	
6 Strong breeze *(39-49 kmph)*	
8 Gale *(62-74 kmph)*	
10 Storm *(89-102 kmph)*	
12 Hurricane *(118 kmph+)*	

A. Wind felt on face, leaves begin to move
B. Everything is destroyed - houses, trees etc.
C. Larger tree branches move   D. Smoke rises vertically
E. Trees blown down, some damage to buildings
F. Whole tree moves, resistance walking against wind

2. Could you invent a scale like this for other weather types or for emotions – tiredness/anger etc? (1 on the happiness scale: 'Corner of mouth turns upwards slightly' etc.)

UNIT 4 SCIENCE, INNOVATION & BUSINESS

PART 4A WORLD ECONOMIES

1. Can you match the country to the economy descriptions?

Saudi Arabia		**1.** World leader in wine exports. The most visited country in the world by tourists
Switzerland		**2.** Leader in car manufacturing & electronic goods. One of Top Three world economies
South Africa		**3.** IT & high tech industries. Agriculture - beef & dairy. Main trade with USA, UK & EU
Japan		**4.** 90% of the economy is based on oil exports
France		**5.** Mining is one of main industries. Leading exporter of diamonds, gold & platinum
Ireland		**6.** A huge part of the economy is based on banking & financial services

2. Can you describe your country's economy? What are the biggest industries/companies?

3. In 1974, Ireland joined the EU and was its poorest member. By 2005, Ireland was ranked as the world's second richest nation. How do you think this happened? *Research the 'Celtic Tiger' and also what happened after 2005.*

4. How does your country's economy rank worldwide? Is it higher or lower than Ireland?

PART 4B HOW PEOPLE DO BUSINESS AROUND THE WORLD

A. *Do you think it's important to understand different cultures if you are doing business? Why?*

TEST WHAT YOU KNOW ABOUT BUSINESS STYLES IN IRELAND AND AROUND THE WORLD

1. An Asian businessman on business in Ireland says, very positively, that his team have lots of good experience working with British companies. The Irish businessman nods his head but doesn't smile.

   a. The deal doesn't happen. Why? **b.** Which communication style below describes the Irish businessman?

A. Good communication is direct, clear and simple with repetition if necessary	
B. Good communication is sophisticated and subtle. Messages are often indirectly suggested	

2. Match the country to what you might do as part of a business negotiation.

A. Bring a small gift from your own country to a meeting B. Sing solo karaoke after dinner C. Do business over vodka D. Go for a lengthy meal E. Have a pint together in the pub				
Japan	**Ireland**	**China**	**Russia**	**Italy**

3. BUSINESS CARDS: Match the correct way to hand someone your business card to the country.

A. No ritual B. Use both hands C. Right hand only	**South Korea**	**UAE**	**Ireland**	

4. LANGUAGE: Where should you apologise for not speaking the local language - in France or Ireland? Why?
5. PUNCTUALITY: Where are business meetings more likely to start late - Ireland or Germany? (Why?)
6. HUMOUR: Where is joking not appreciated during a business meeting - Sweden or Ireland? (Why?)
7. Which of the following statements are True/False about working or doing business in Ireland?

	T/F
A. Irish are informal. Employees and managers will use first names and may socialise together	
B. Business in Ireland is so fast-paced that there is often no time for pre-business small talk	
C. Personal relationships are valued more than corporate ones and are vital for business success	

8. Which of these statements are True/False?

	T/F
A. In negotiations, Irish will listen quietly and take a moment's silence before responding	
B. Many women hold strong roles in Irish business and may often lead a negotiating team	
C. Direct confrontation or criticism are common and will not negatively affect relationships	

B. *What advice would you give somebody doing business in your country? Make a list of Dos & Don'ts.*
C. *Would any aspects of how Irish people do business be seen negatively in your country?*

ON YOUR OWN

1. MARKET YOUR NATION: Eg. *Ireland: Land of history and possibilities.* Write a slogan to market your country with.
2. Play 'The International Trading Game' in class. (See ONLINE SECTION.)
3. Visit the Science gallery or Collin's Barracks Science museum in Dublin. Or an Irish science/business fair.
4. Research an inventor, scientist or business entrepreneur you admire. Make a presentation on them to your class.

WARM UP

1. Do you like art? Are you good at drawing or painting?
2. What visual symbols best represent your country? What is your country's most famous work of art/most famous building?
3. Who are your country's biggest fashion icons?
4. What visual symbols would you most associate with Ireland?

PART 1 IRISH ART HISTORY

1. What is your most valued personal possession? Why?
2. Do you have any possession (phone/bag/helmet etc.) that you've personalised? Why do you think we decorate objects in this way?
3. Match the Irish artefacts below to the pictures and descriptions.

ARTEFACT	1	2	3	4	5	6	7	8
PICTURE								
DESCRIPTION								

> **1.** Megalithic Stone, 3000 BC **2.** Gleninsheen Collar, 700 BC
> **3.** Loughnashade Horn, 100 BC **4.** Tara Brooch, 750 AD
> **5.** Ardagh Chalice (Cup), 800 AD **6.** Balinderry Sword, 850 AD
> **7.** Book of Kells, 9th Century **8.** Durrow Cross, 10th Century

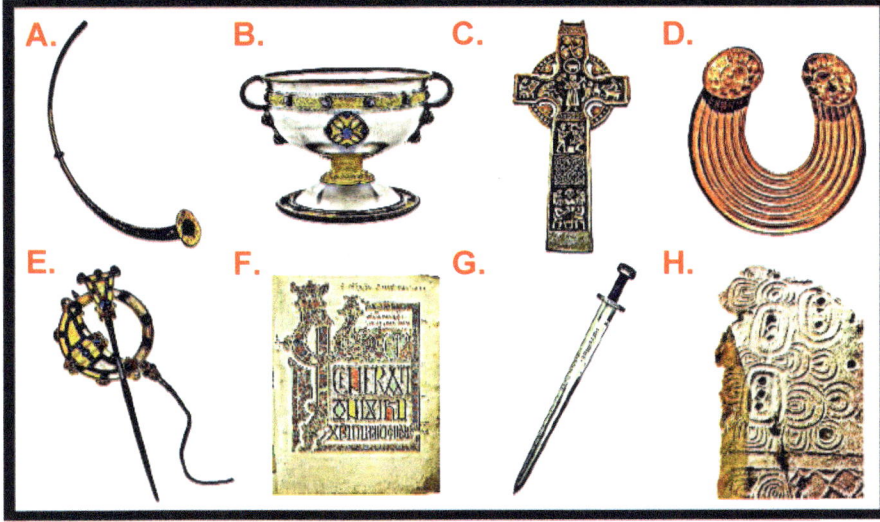

A.   B.   C.   D.
E.   F.   G.   H.

***i.** An illustrated Latin manuscript created in a monastery*
***ii.** Iron Age. Noise was used by Celts in battle to scare enemies*
***iii.** Early Medieval. Highly decorated jewellery worn on clothes*
***iv.** Neolithic Age. Abstract spirals on stone*
***v.** Important weapon used by invading Vikings*
***vi.** Religious stonework possibly linking Pagan sun-god & Christ*
***vii.** Early Christian decorated silver. Held wine during Mass*
***viii.** Bronze Age metalwork. Gold neck decoration for rich man*

4. **HISTORY TEST:** Use the information above to help you answer.
   A. Can you put the time periods in chronological order?

	Iron Age		*Medieval*		*Bronze Age*		*Neolithic*

   B. Which came to Ireland first - Christianity or the Vikings?
   C. Ireland's artistic 'golden age' (Celtic/early Christian period) happened partly because Ireland <u>wasn't</u> invaded by who?
   D. Who <u>did</u> invade in 1169 causing a long artistic decline?

5. Has your country had a 'golden age' of art?
6. TASK: Design your own personalised object (jewellery, a wallet, shoes, a pen etc.) Explain your design decisions to the class.

Share your genuine feelings about the quotes... join the discussion. Can you share any similar quotes from your own culture?

ART
But is it art?

UNIT 5 VISUAL IRELAND

PART 2A IRISH ARCHITECTURE

1. What is your favourite building? What's the ugliest building you can think of?
2. Can you put the Irish buildings below from different historical periods in the correct chronological order? Match the pictures and building names to the correct time period/architectural style.

TIME/ARCHITECTURAL STYLE	PICTURE	BUILDING		IRISH BUILDINGS
12th Century 'Romanesque'				A. Bellamont Country House, Cavan
18th Century 'Palladian'				B. Drive-thru restaurant, Galway
19th Century 'Victorian'				C. Norman Castle, Trim
20th Century 'Brutalist'				D. Government Building, Cork
21st Century 'Contemporary'				E. National Museum, Dublin

3. 'Ireland has a complicated relationship with its historic buildings.' Why? Can you explain this statement?
4. Which is your favourite architectural style above? Why? Find out more about it. What did a typical building look like in your country in the same period? Compare some visual examples with your class.

PART 2B CITYSCAPES

1. What is your favourite city in the world? Why? Can you match the famous skylines below to the cities?

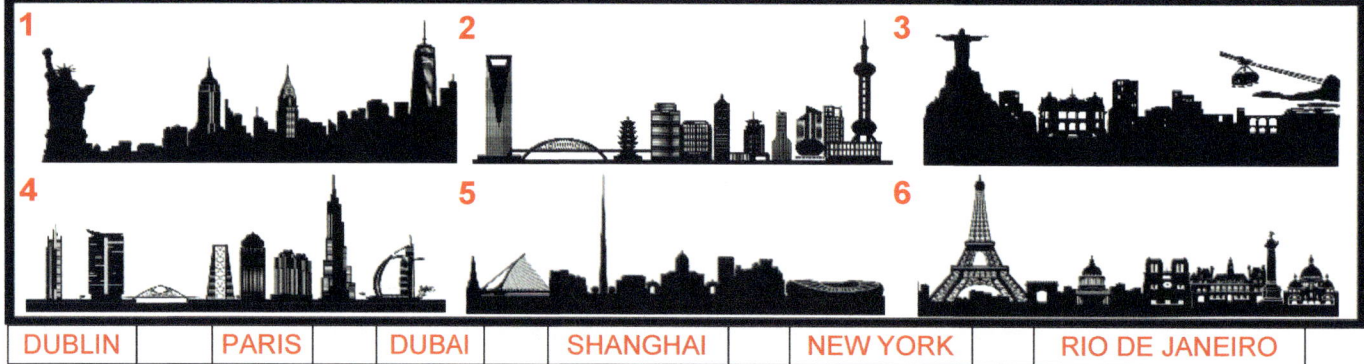

DUBLIN		PARIS		DUBAI		SHANGHAI		NEW YORK		RIO DE JANEIRO	

2. What makes a well-designed city? How are Irish cities/towns designed differently from your country?
3. **TASK 1:** Design a building to fit in with a specific location near you. *(Think about colour, material etc.)* **Or…**
   TASK 2: Design your perfect city. *(Think about location, transport, climate, building style etc.)*

PART 2C YOUR DREAM HOME

1. How is your house in your country different from typical Irish houses?
2. Match the Descriptions and Pictures to the Countries on the bottom right.

A. South-facing windows. Slanted roof. Chimney. Shelter over door
B. Slanted roof. Chimney. Gutter pipes. Large windows
C. Built on posts. Slanted roof. Open windows. lots of air circulation
D. Flat roof. Thick walls. Small windows or balconies. Lots of shade

3. 1 and 3 are made of stone. 2 and 4 of wood. Can you think of reasons why?
4. Which house is best for each climate below? Give reasons why.

a. Hot & humid. Risk of flooding	b. Rainy. Cold. Dark in winter
c. Lots of snow. Cold. Bright sunshine	d. Hot & dry. Very strong sun

SWEDEN		EGYPT	
THAILAND		IRELAND	

5. **TASK:** Design your perfect house.

PART 3A WHAT'S YOUR IMAGE?

1. Do you think a lot about what you wear? What fashions do you love? Or hate?
2. Has your style changed over time? Do you have any embarrassing fashion mistakes from your past?
3.
> *Jewellery - Hats - Tattoos - Piercings - Hairstyle - Clothes - Facial Hair - Sunglasses - Makeup*

In PART 1 we saw how the *Tara brooch* and *Gleninsheen collar* were worn to show social status.
In the modern world, what information might the things in the box above communicate about someone? *(Eg. Job, attitude, religion, politics, social class, hobbies, lifestyle, nationality etc.)*
4. In pairs, say what messages the 'fashion statements' in the pictures communicate about each person.

5. How would you describe your own image? What do you think you communicate through your style?
6. How do you dress differently in different situations? *(Eg. Meeting friends vs. A job interview)* Do you think changing clothes can change your behavior and/or the behavior of others towards you?
7. Can you think of a situation where the meaning of clothes could be misunderstood between cultures?

PART 3B IRISH FASHION

i. Which countries are the most stylish? Do you think your country has better/worse fashion than Ireland?
2. Which of the styles by Irish fashion designers in the pictures do you like most? Why?
In pairs, choose two adjectives to describe each style.

> *Simple - (un)fashionable - casual - classic - sporty*
> *elegant - comfortable - formal - revealing*
> *tight/loose-fitting - modest - smart - sensible - vintage*
> *trendy - cute - scruffy - dressed to kill - practical*
> *(un)conventional - sophisticated - traditional - young*
> *mature - modern - old-fashioned - glamorous*
> *distinctive - graceful - flamboyant - tacky*

3. Research the famous Irish womenswear designers: *Paul Costello, Louise Kennedy, Phillip Treacy, Lainey Keogh, Peter O'Brien* and model *Anne Gunning*. Could you match each to the pictures (1-6)?
4. **A.** *'Irish street style has lots of individuality and creativity.'*
   B. *'Irish often pretend not to care how they look, even if they do care a lot.'* Do you agree with these statements? How would you describe the attitude to fashion in your country?
5. **TASK:** Design a perfect outfit for an Irish night out.

PART 3C WHAT COLOUR ARE YOU?

1. Are the colours Irish people wear different from your country? What do you think affects colour choice in clothes?
2. What colours do you usually wear? Match the colours below with what each says about your personality.

A. Red B. Grey *C. Yellow* D. Green E. Blue *F. Brown* G. White H. Black

You're calm, peaceful & loyal	You are reliable, home-loving & practical
You're bright, optimistic & logical	You're innocent, good-natured & organised
You're balanced, social & warm-hearted	You don't want to be the centre of attention
You're passionate, active & enthusiastic	You are mysterious & powerful

3. Do you agree with the descriptions above? Do the colours you wear depend on your mood?

PART 4 MODERN IRISH PAINTING

1. Do you like galleries/museums? What's the best one you've visited? Have you been to any in Ireland?
2. **TASK 1:** List ways to improve the 'gallery experience' to get young people to engage more with art.
3. Who is your country's most famous artist? Who is your own favourite artist?
4. **TASK 2:** Look out the window. How would you paint the scene? Would the colours/materials etc. that you use change depending on the country you're in? Make notes and a sketch plan for your painting.
5. Fine art paintings are traditionally divided into five categories. Match the ten Irish works of art in the pictures with a category in the grid below on the left. *(There are two paintings in each category.)*

A *William Scott*	B *Seán Keating*	C *Roderic O'Conor*	D *William Orpen*	E *James Barry*
F *Louis Le Brocquy*	G *Norah McGuinness*	H *Robert Ballagh*	I *Francis Bacon*	J *Jack B. Yeats*

THE FIVE ART CATEGORIES			ART MOVEMENTS
1. History - Religious/historical painting with a moral message			**Neoclassicism**
2. Portraits - Individual, group or self			**Academy Art – Minimalism Realism – Fauvism**
3. Genre - Scenes telling a story of everyday life			**Expressionism – Cubism**
4. Landscape - Principal content is a countryside view			**Pop Art – Surrealism**
5. Still Life - Domestic or everyday objects			**Impressionism**

6. Look at the Art Styles/Movements in the box on the right. Have you heard of any of them? What do you think they mean? *Ask your teacher or check the ONLINE SECTION for more information on each.*
7. Look up examples of each style online. Can you find any works by famous international artists or artists from your country in each style? Are any of these paintings similar to the Irish ones above?
8. Can you identify which Irish paintings in each category from above are in which specific artistic style?

HISTORY PAINTING		PORTRAITS		GENRE PAINTING		LANDSCAPES		STILL LIFE	
Pop Art		*Cubist*		*Expressionist*		*Impressionist*		*Surrealist*	
Neoclassical		*Academy Art*		*Realist*		*Fauvist*		*Minimalist*	

9. Which is your favourite/least favourite painting above? Find out more about the artist that you like most. What were his/her influences? What do you think he/she is trying to say in the painting above?
10. **TASK 3:** Draw a picture in one of the artistic styles. Compare your final work with the other students.

ON YOUR OWN

1. Visit the National/Modern/Hugh Lane gallery, Dublin, the Crawford gallery, Cork or other galleries around Ireland.
2. Attend one of Ireland's many arts festivals: Galway, Carlow, Clonmel, Waterford, 'Earagail' etc.
3. Visit the 'Fashion Exhibition' at Collins Barracks or National Craft centres like Clarecastle or Kilkenny.
4. Design a plan for a study or library space within your school.
5. Dress like an Irish person. See how it feels. Do you feel different? Do people behave differently towards you?
6. Design a smartphone app. Describe what it does and give reasons for your design decisions.
7. Walk around an Irish city/town. Look at the buildings. Choose one you like and one you don't. Report back.

WARM UP

1. Why do you think we create legends? How do they start?
2. Who is the most famous legendary character in your culture?
3. What was your favourite fairy story as a child?
4. Do you like modern fantasy books or films? What is your favourite? Who is your favourite superhero?

PART 1 ARCHETYPAL CHARACTERS

1. Can you match the typical character types in legends and mythology in the box to the pictures and the descriptions?

CHARACTER TYPE	1	2	3	4	5	6	7	8
PICTURE								
DESCRIPTION								

1. The Action Girl 2. The Mentor 3. The Seductress
4. The Jealous Queen 5. The Hero/Warrior 6. The Trickster
7. The Friendly Monster 8. The Shadow/Enemy

A. He shows selfless courage and strength for the greater good

B. She is independent-minded, rebellious and fights for freedom

C. He is wise and knowledgeable. He teaches and guides the hero

D. She uses beauty and sensual charm to get what she wants

E. The monster, the threat to the hero, the scary part of life

F. He has important knowledge. But can you trust him?

G. She is cold-hearted, insecure, powerful and dangerous

H. It serves the hero and shows the side of nature that helps us

2. Think of examples of the characters above in modern stories.
3. Write your own description for any three of the typical character types in the box below and give a modern example.

Damsel in distress -- anti-hero -- animal companion
dangerous rival -- tyrant king -- wanderer -- chosen one

iv. Some believe that dragon legends began with early humans finding dinosaur bones. In pairs, choose one of the creatures below and imagine how its legend might have begun.

Half-human/half-animal -- undead -- shape-shifters
faery folk -- witches -- giants

Share your genuine feelings about the quotes… join the discussion. Can you share any similar quotes from your own culture?

I am a legend. If you don't believe me, just ask me.

IRISH LAKE GIANT

PART 2A IRISH HEROES: CÚ CHULAINN & FIONN MACCUMHAILL

1. Work in pairs, each read one of the stories about the two most famous hero warriors of Irish legend, *Cú Chulainn* and *Fionn MacCumhaill*. Then tell your partner the three most interesting things you learned.

CÚ CHULAINN, the son of Deichtine and the god Lugh, was born at Newgrange. When he was seven, the magician, Cathbad, told him that any boy who used weapons that day would be famous forever. Cú Chulainn took up the weapons of his uncle Conchobar, the King of Ulster, but Cathbad then finished his prophecy saying this boy would also have a short life. When Cú Chulainn was sixteen, Queen Medb of Connacht attacked Ulster to steal their best bull. Ulster was under a curse stopping its men from fighting so Cú Chulainn challenged the whole Connacht army. They refused to fight a 'beardless boy'. Cú Chulainn ran off, shaved a goat and made a fake beard before returning to defeat the whole Connacht army at Cooley. When Cú Chulainn fought, he became a monstrous creature. His legs twisted backwards, his eyes popped out and his mouth opened to his ribs. After one battle, his friends surrounded him with beautiful women. When he turned away in embarrassment, they threw him into a bath of water to calm him. The bath exploded. Cú Chulainn wished to marry Emer but her father Forgall said he must first train in Scotland with the warrior-woman, Scáthach. Forgall expected Cú Chulainn to be killed but when Cú Chulainn fought Scáthach, they were equal. Cú Chulainn eventually got control and forced her to have his son. While she was pregnant, he returned to Ireland, killed Forgall and married Emer. Eight years later, Scáthach sent the young Connla to Ireland in secret. Cú Chulainn killed him, realising only at the last moment it was his son. On his way to fight a group of men, Cú Chulainn met the Morrigan, three one-eyed old women, eating roast dog. They invited him to join them. Cú Chulainn had two curses which, if broken, would lead to his death - never to refuse hospitality and never to eat dog. He had no choice but to eat and it made him weak. When he was later wounded at Knockbridge, he tied himself to a stone so he would die facing his enemies.

FIONN MACCUMHAILL was the son of Cumhaill who was killed by Goll Mac Morna, the leader of a group of warriors, the Fianna. Cumhaill's wife Muirne was pregnant with Fionn and she escaped into exile. Fionn grew up in secret in the forests of the Slieve Bloom mountains not knowing who his parents were. He was trained by the woman warrior Liath. She taught him to hunt and fight. Fionn served many local kings, but often his secret past forced him to leave and travel again. Fionn studied under the magic druid Finnegas who was searching for the 'salmon of knowledge' in the Boyne river. Eventually the old man caught it and told Fionn to cook it for him. While cooking, Fionn burned his thumb on the fish and accidentally put his thumb in his mouth, gaining the salmon's wisdom. With his new knowledge, Fionn understood who he was and how to fight back against Goll. Every year a faery, Aillen, came to Tara, the home of the High Kings, as a beautiful woman. She made the Fianna warriors fall asleep with sensual music. Aillen then changed into a fire-breathing monster and burned down the palace. Fionn arrived and put his spear against his forehead so the pain kept him awake through the music. He killed Aillen. Fionn replaced Goll as leader of the Fianna. Fionn's first wife was Sadbh who'd been turned into a deer by a magician. Fionn hunted her but did not kill her and she immediately changed into a beautiful woman. They had a son, Oisín. Later, Sadbh was changed back into a deer and vanished into the forest. Fionn once threw a piece of land into the sea at an enemy. The hole left behind became Lough Neagh. Fionn also created the Giant's Causeway as stepping stones from Ireland to Scotland. When Fionn learned that the Scottish giant Benandonner wanted to fight him, Fionn knew he couldn't win so he asked his new wife Oona to dress him as a baby. When Benandonner arrived and saw how big and strong the 'baby' was, he got scared and ran back to Scotland.

2. Can you find these places mentioned in the stories on a modern map of Ireland?

Newgrange – Cooley – Knockbridge – Slieve Bloom – Boyne River – Lough Neagh – Giant's Causeway

3. Match the character types on the left with the specific characters on the right from the legends above.

1. Action Girl 2. Mentor 3. Seductress 4. Trickster 5. Dangerous Rival 6. Anti-hero 7. Witches 8. Shape-shifter 9. Dragon 10. Wanderer	A. Fionn B. Cú Chulainn C. Scáthach (& Liath) D. Aillen x 2 E. Finnegas (& Liath) F. Sadbh (& Aillen) G. Cathbad H. Benandonner (& Goll) I. The Morrigan

1	2	3	4	5	6	7	8	9	10

4. Myths reflect a culture's beliefs and morals. What do you think of the behaviour and society of the two heroes?
5. Do you learn the legends of your country as children? Can you share one with your class?

UNIT 6 IRISH MYTHS & LEGENDS

PART 2B TYPICAL LEGEND THEMES

1. Write a brief summary of the story of a modern fantasy/superhero film or book that you like.
2. Typical themes often reappear in legends around the world as well as in fantasy/superhero stories. Match the themes with the parts of the *Cú Chulainn/Fionn* stories, the modern stories and the pictures.

THEME	IRISH LEGEND	MODERN STORY	PICTURE	IRISH LEGEND
Task to win love				**1.** Cú Chulainn & Cathbad
Fighting the monster				**2.** Fionn in Slieve Bloom
Hero's hidden origins				**3.** Cú Chulainn & Emer
The chosen one				**4.** Fionn & Goll
Bad disguise				**5.** Fionn & Aillen
Hero's revenge				**6.** Cú Chulainn & the goat / Fionn the baby

MODERN STORY	
	A. They must stop Skynet and the terminators and save the people - **Terminator**
	B. Lord Farquaad sends Shrek to rescue Princess Fiona, expecting him to be killed - **Shrek**
	C. As foretold in the prophesy, Neo is the One who will destroy the Matrix - **The Matrix**
	D. Clark Kent puts on a pair of glasses and somehow people don't recognise him - **Superman**
	E. Rey grows up in exile not knowing her family, maybe for her own protection - **Star Wars**
	F. William Wallace is motivated by anger against the English who killed his wife - **Braveheart**

i ii iii iv v vi

Other typical legend themes include: divine battles / tests of strength / the voyage / an army of super soldiers / death and rebirth / apocalypse / forbidden romance… (You'll find all these in Irish mythology.)

3. Look back at the legend from your country you mentioned in *PART 2A.v* and/or at your summary of a fantasy/superhero story above in *Exercise i*. Can you identify any of these themes in your stories?
4. **TASK:** In pairs/small groups, create your own legend story. Compare your finished stories.

PART 3A WHY WE CREATE MYTHS & LEGENDS

1. Can you rank these four explanations why myths are created in order of importance (1–4)? Give reasons.

	Explain the origins of the culture		Explain the world, nature & strange happenings
	Provide moral guidance		Pass on oral history of long ago battles, events & people

2. Can you think of any myths or legends in your culture that fulfil any of these roles? Share them with the class.
3. In the modern world, do we still use stories or superstitions to explain things we don't understand? Give examples.
4. Where do we find moral guidance in the modern world? Is it better than the old legends?

PART 3B THE OTHERWORLD

Like most cultures, Irish legends deal a lot with the 'otherworld', with gods and magical beings. The inhabitants of Ireland before the Gaels/Irish were the Tuatha Dé Danann. They were immortal, intelligent, magical faery folk who'd previously won a 'divine conflict' for control of Ireland with the Fomorians, sea-faring giants. When the Irish arrived, the Tuatha disappeared underground but they still had a big influence on people's lives.

1. 'It wasn't a good idea to make the faery folk angry.' What do you think might happen if you did?
2. You could find the faeries through special, secret 'gateways'. Some legends describe journeys into the spirit world. Why would people travel to the spirit world? (Would you?)
3. Are there stories of faery people in your culture? Have you ever seen one? Would you like to?

PART 4 'LABHRAIDH LOINGSEACH'

1. Look at the picture of Labhraidh Loinseach. He was once a legendary High King of Ireland. You might notice that he has horse's ears. In pairs/small groups, think up answers to the questions below.

1.	*How did Labhraidh get his horse's ears?*
2.	*How did he keep his ears secret?*
3.	*What was the problem with getting his hair cut?*
4.	*What do you think happened to all his hairdressers?*
5.	*What did one hairdresser offer Labhraidh that he couldn't resist?*
6.	*Where did the hairdresser finally go to whisper the secret?*
7.	*Why did the king want to have a big celebration after ten years?*
8.	*Where did the musician go to find material to make a new harp?*
9.	*What happened when the musician played the harp at the celebration?*
10.	*How did the king react?*

2. Compare answers with other groups. Ask your teacher or check the ONLINE SECTION for the full story.
3. In Greek mythology, King Midas also had horse's ears. Do you think this is just a coincidence?

PART 5 'THE CHILDREN OF LIR' & 'OISÍN IN TÍR NA NÓG'

1. Read the two legends below and match the titles with the correct story. Some may go with both.

A. The myth of Eternal Youth *B. The Jealous Queen* *C. St. Patrick arrives* *D. More shape-shifters* *E. Journey into the spirit world* *F. Faery magic* *G. Romantic vs family love*	LIR	OISÍN	BOTH

CHILDREN OF LIR: *King Lir had a beautiful wife Eva and four children - a son Aodh, a daughter Fionnula and twin boys, Fiachra and Conn. Eva died when the children were young. Lir remarried with Eva's sister Aoife. Aoife resented the King's love for his children. She wanted all of his attention for herself. One day, she took the children to swim in a lake. Aoife used her*  *magic powers to turn them all into swans, forcing them to live for three hundred years on the lake, three hundred on the Seas of Moyle and three hundred more on the Isle of Inish Glora. The magic spell would only be broken when the children heard the ringing of St. Patrick's bell. Aoife's magic had not taken away the children's voices and so they were able to tell their father what had happened. Furious, Lir changed Aoife into a mist and she was never seen again. Lir spent his days by the lake listening to his children singing. After three hundred years, the swans had to go to the seas of Moyle, experiencing cold and fierce storms. They survived nine hundred sad years, finally heard a bell ringing and changed back into humans. The children, now old, were taken to a church and blessed before they died.*

TÍR NA NÓG: *One day Oisín and his father Fionn Mac Cumhaill were hunting when they saw a beautiful, mysterious young woman approaching on a white horse. "I'm Niamh," she said. "My father is King of Tír Na nÓg, a land without sadness, where nobody gets old. I've come to take Oisín with me." Oisín immediately fell in love and agreed to go with her but promising to return soon. The horse ran far across the seas to the magical land. There, Niamh and Oisín spent many happy times, although part of Oisín's heart still missed Ireland. Finally, Oisín asked Niamh to let him return. For him it was only a few years, but back in Ireland over three hundred years had passed. Niamh said, "Take my horse but don't let your feet touch the ground or you won't return." Oisín rode across the sea and arrived to find everything changed in Ireland. He met some weak-looking men trying to move a huge rock. He leant down from his horse to help them, but lost his balance and fell. Immediately, Oisín changed into an old man. The horse ran away. Oisín asked for his father but the men said Fionn had died many years before. Oisín was broken-hearted and was taken to meet St. Patrick and blessed before he died.*

ii. Are there any similar legends in your culture of: **A.** faery curses **B.** journeys into the spirit world **C.** a land of eternal youth? Do you think we still look for myths of eternal youth in modern culture?
iii. Why does St. Patrick appear at the end of each legend? Do you think he was always in the stories?
iv. Would you leave your life and everything you know for love like Oisín? Why/why not?
v. Of the three stories above, which is your favourite? Why?

ON YOUR OWN

1. Read more about Irish legends or watch a film about Irish legends like 'The Song of the Sea'.
2. Invent a legend to explain: Why it rains in Ireland? Why Irish have red hair? How the Irish invented whiskey? Etc.
3. Visit Tara. Or Newgrange. Or other ancient places associated with legends in Ireland.

WARM UP

1. When you're learning a foreign language, do you think it is important to learn about the culture and character of the people who speak the language? Why/Why not?
2. Language is an important part of our identity. Can you give any examples in your own language of words, expressions or pronunciations that identify people as coming from a specific area or city in your country?
3. Can you notice anything specific in how Irish speak English? (Vocabulary, pronunciation etc.)

PART 1 ACCENTS IN ENGLISH

1. What is your favourite accent in your own language? Why?
2. Look at the tongue twister below and read it out loud.

> *Betty bought a bit of butter but the bit of butter Betty bought was bitter, so Betty bought a better bit of butter to make her bitter butter better.*

3. Listen to the three recordings. Can you say which accent is an English accent, which one is Irish and which is American?
ONLINE SECTION - Audio File 7.1.A.

Listening 1	
Listening 2	
Listening 3	

What are the specific pronunciation differences between each accent? Focus on the '*t*', '*r*' and vowel sounds.

4. What do you think is the most difficult accent in English to understand? Why? Do you have a favourite accent?
5. **Audio File 7.1.B.** Listen to the tongue twister in three different Irish accents. How is the '*t*' sound different in each one? Match each to the correct listening: **A.** *Sounds like an American 't'* **B.** *'t' is silent* **C.** *'t' is an 'sh' sound*

Listening 4	
Listening 5	
Listening 6	

What else can you notice about the Irish accent? What about the '*th*' sound in 'the' or the pronunciation of 'a'?

6. **Audio File 7.1.C.** One generally consistent feature of the all accents above is a rising/falling intonation pattern. Listen to three non-native speakers. Match each Listening to a Nationality: **A.** *Moroccan (Arabic)* **B.** *Russian* **C.** *Spanish*. What can you notice about the intonation/ pronunciation of each that differs from a native speaker?

Listening 7	
Listening 8	
Listening 9	

7. How do you think your own accent/pronunciation sounds in English compared to a native speaker? What is your biggest pronunciation difficulty in English?
8. And finally, Ireland was once voted the 'World's Sexiest Accent'. Do you agree? Give reasons for or against.

QUOTES

Which is your favourite quote? Why?

"A man with an Irish accent can sound wise & interesting & poetic... even when he isn't..."
– Kate Atkinson

"Language is the clothes in which your thoughts walk in public." **– George Crane**

"The great thing about how English is spoken in Ireland is that it perfectly reflects the Irish character." **– Mark Barr**

"Kindness is the language that the deaf can hear & the blind can see." **– Mark Twain**

"Slang is the poetry of the poor man."
– John Moore

"The limits of my language are the limits of my world." **– Wittgenstein**

"The English language like all languages is a work in progress. Have fun with it!"
– Jonathon Culver

"The English language is the property of nobody but the imagination." **– Derek Walcott**

"A different language is a different vision of life." **– Federico Fellini**

"My accent works on girls. They like it. I've no idea why." **– Niall Horan. One Direction**

SAYINGS TRANSLATED FROM IRISH

"Broken Irish is better than clever English."
"Bad deeds return on the bad-deed doer."
"A light heart lives longest."
"The work praises the man."
"A fool & his money are soon parted."
"A good start is half the work."

Share your genuine feelings about the quotes... join the discussion. Can you share any similar quotes from your own culture?

I have t'ree brothers.

What do you mean - your brothers live in a forest?!

PART 2 ENGLISH AROUND THE WORLD

Accent is not the only thing that is different in how English is spoken around the world. There can also be variations of vocabulary, expression and even of grammar.

1. Look at the two sentences below. The first one can be heard in many parts of England. The second is a very common American usage. Can you change them back into standard grammatical English?

1. 'I was stood at the bus stop for two hours.'	**2.** 'I ain't gonna listen to a thing he says.'

2. Look at the famous people below using expressions from the country where they come from.
    Can you match each colloquial expression with the place it comes from and with the meaning?

i Gareth Bale, footballer — *Our new team shirts are lush.*

ii Charlize Theron, actress — *Mmm, that was lekker.*

iii Bob Marley, singer — *Hey, man. You criss?*

iv Peter Jackson, director — *I'm stoked about my new film.*

v Van Morrison, singer — *'Bout ye?*

vi Rakesh Sharma astronaut — *Hmm, I'm feeling glassy.*

vii Elle MacPherson, model — *G'day mate.*

viii Drake, rapper — *Whaddya at, eh?*

ix Andy Murray tennis player — *Och, nae bother, laddie.*

PLACES

A. South Africa
B. New Zealand
C. Australia
D. India
E. Canada
F. Wales
G. Northern Ireland
H. Scotland
I. Jamaica

MEANINGS

1. Excited (Adj)
2. What are you doing?
3. Thirsty (Adj)
4. How are you?
5. Hello friend
6. No problem, young man
7. Are you OK?
8. Lovely (Adj)
9. Delicious (Adj)

EXPRESSION	i	ii	iii	iv	v	vi	vii	viii	ix
PLACE									
MEANING									

3. Write down two examples of expressions you like in English. Why do you like them?
4. Translate two expressions you like from your language. Can you find similar expressions in English?

PART 3A ENGLISH IN IRELAND – OLD & MIDDLE

1. One influence on Irish English is the continued use of words from Old (500-1000 AD) and Middle English (1100-1500 AD) that have died out in other parts of the world. Can you explain the words below from the context of the sentence?

"**Tis** a fine day today." *(Old English)*	
"What is that **yoke** you have in your hand?" *(Old English)*	
"Why did you **mitch** class yesterday?" asked the teacher angrily. *(Middle English)*	
"**Whisht**! I want to listen to this." *(Middle English)*	

2. Any ideas or theories why these older forms still exist in Irish English even though they are no longer used in England? Do you (or any other group of speakers) use any older forms in your own language?

UNIT 7 HOW IRISH SPEAK

PART 3B ENGLISH IN IRELAND - *AS GAEILGE*

1. Probably the most important influence on how English is used in Ireland comes from the native Irish language - *Gaeilge*. Read the six facts about the Irish language below. Which one surprises you most?

FACTS ABOUT THE IRISH LANGUAGE
1. Irish has no words for 'yes' and 'no'. Instead, we repeat the verb used in the question.
2. In Irish we use 'after + …ing' for a recently completed action. *('Tá mé tar éis…')*
3. In Irish, there are different words for 'you singular' and 'you plural'. *('Tu' and 'Sibh')*
4. There is no verb 'to have'. For possession, use 'to be' plus 'with me' or 'on me'. *('Tá … agam/orm')*
5. The use of 'bring' and 'take' is decided by the person saying it rather than the direction. *('Beir' and 'Tóg')*
6. The verb 'to be' has two different present tenses, for 'things that are generally true' *('Tá sé')* and for 'habitual actions' *('Bíonn sé')*. The 'habitual action' tense can be roughly translated as 'do be doing'.

COMPARING LANGUAGES. In Irish, having different words for 'you singular' and 'you plural' would seem to be better, clearer than English. However, not having a verb 'to have' would seem to be a disadvantage. Do you agree?

In your own language, can you think of any elements of grammar or vocabulary, similar to above, that are different from English? Are those differences better or worse? Or just different?

IRISH TOILETS

Hmm... which one?

PART 3C CORRECT THE 'MISTAKES'

1. If your teacher is Irish, now is your chance to correct him/her. The sentences contain constructions you might hear in spoken Irish English. Can you 'correct' the sentences back into more standard English?

A. I'm doing it wrong, amn't I?	
B. Where's me mobile? It was on me a minute ago.	
C. What does he be doing up there in his room?	
D. Damn! I'm after losing my keys.	
E. What are ye doing for the weekend?	
F. Don't forget to bring your umbrella with you when you leave.	
G. 'Is he coming home soon?' 'He is.'	
H. Youse don't understand anything.	

2. Two of the sentences above use variations of Old English forms for 'you plural'. Which two sentences?
3. Look back up at PART 3B. Which sentence 'mistakes' are linked to which 'Facts about the Irish language'?

PART 4A MAKE THE LANGUAGE YOUR OWN

1. Irish English is not just about a few grammar differences. It's about the character and individuality of the people. **Match the expressions below with the (we think less elegant) standard English forms on the right.**

A. *Good man yourself. Fair play to ya!*	Any news?	
B. *Well, how's she cuttin'?*	Poor you	
C. *Take care! Don't work too hard!*	To complain *(v)*	
D. *He's always giving out.*	How are you?	
E. *Story?*	Goodbye	
F. *My car is banjaxed.*	Idiot *(n)*	
G. *God love ya!*	Well done	
H. *He's a gobshite, an eejit.*	Broken *(adj)*	

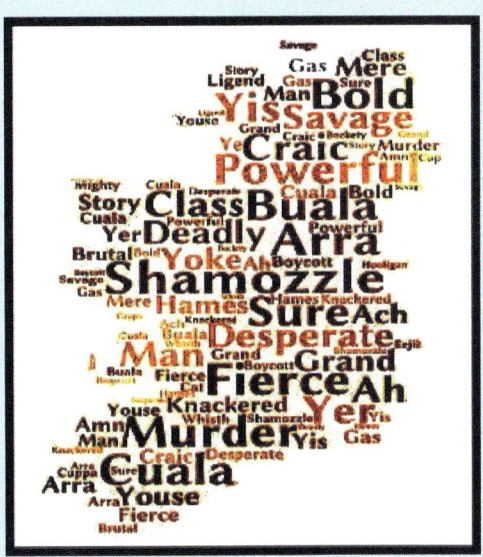

PART 4B 'I'M GRAND'

1. How do Irish people typically answer the question, *'How are you?'*
2. If an Irish person answers *'I'm grand'*, what do they mean? (Does it depend a lot on the facial expression and tone of voice?)
3. Irish people are generally quite non-confrontational. If an Irish person disagrees with you, they will be diplomatic. They'll sometimes just become silent or give a vague answer rather than saying 'no' directly. Can you think of positive/negative aspects of this way of behaviour?
4. How about you - are you more diplomatic or direct?
5. Showing modesty and a lack of arrogance are also important in Ireland. Irish people are often not good at accepting compliments. How about you? How do you react when someone compliments you?

"Hi, I'm the English language and I don't always play by the rules!"

6. **Match the statements on the left to the *modest* or *indirect* answers on the right.**

A. 'Thank you very much.'	*'Hmm, yeah, I see what you mean, eh…' (IE 'No')*
B. Waiter: 'How is your meal?'	*'Ah, she's grand. She'll do.'*
C. 'Well done. You did a great job.'	*'Stop, it was no bother.'*
D. 'Are you coming to the party?'	*'Eh, yeah it's… fine.' (IE 'It's not fine')*
E. 'You look really well.'	*'It's going slowly. I'm surviving. Just.'*
F. 'How's it going?'	*'I just did my best. It wasn't that complicated.'*
G. 'Do you agree?'	*'Eh, yeah… I might see you there.' (IE 'No')*
H. 'Your girlfriend is lovely.'	*'Well?! Are you joking me? I look awful.'*

7. Have you experienced Irish people being *indirect* or *modest* in this way when they speak?
8. Is this Irish way different from, or similar to, your culture? Think about how people from your country express themselves if they disagree, want to complain, are praised etc. Compare with other students.

PART 5 'THAT'S LOVELY'

1. Irish people use the words 'nice' and 'lovely' all the time to describe many different things. Think of some more expressive words to use instead in the examples below. Use Suggestions from the box or your own words.

Very NICE

It's *lovely* weather today.	
It was so *nice* of you to come and visit us.	
Your new dress is really *lovely*.	
He's a *nice* man.	
That music is really *lovely*.	
She's not the most fashionable but she looks *nice*.	
I live in a *lovely* little house.	
They look *nice* together.	
Irish people are generally *nice*.	
I had a *lovely* time on holiday.	

SUGGESTIONS

*Colourful
Charming - Kind
Sunny - Welcoming
Pretty - Generous - Cute
Attractive - Exquisite
Cosy - Warm - Relaxing
Bright - Enjoyable
Beautiful - Sweet
Gorgeous - Friendly
Thoughtful*

ON YOUR OWN

1. Here are some Irish language words you might have seen. Do you know what any of them mean? Look them up.

    Fáilte – Gardai – An lár – Fir – Mná – Sláinte

2. Would you like to speak with an Irish accent? Or like the Queen? Or the US president? Think about how you'd like your own English to sound. What is important to you? Record yourself speaking in English and listen back.
3. Find out more about different varieties of English – South African. Scottish. Jamaican etc. Report back to the class.
4. Do you feel 'different' in a different language? Think about when you speak English – do you move your body or even think a little bit differently from in your own language?

UNIT 8 HOW IRISH MOVE

WARM UP

1. Do you like dancing? Are you good? Where do you go dancing?
2. In general, are people from your country good dancers?
3. How important do you think body language is when you are communicating with someone? Can you give an example of when understanding body language is important?

PART 1 GESTURES QUIZ

Test what you know about gestures from around the world.

1. In what country is it rude to sit showing the soles of the feet?
   A. Ireland
   B. Canada
   C. Vietnam
   D. Colombia

2. In Ireland, pointing, scrunching your face and raising your voice make you seem angry. In Kenya, what will people think?
   A. You are happy
   B. You are singing
   C. You are saying hello to them
   D. You have mental problems

3. In Ireland, when taking a photo, people sometimes make the 'rabbit ears' sign behind another person's head as a joke. If you do it to a Brazilian or Italian man, what are you saying?
   A. That he is going bald
   B. That he is a bad person
   C. That his wife is cheating on him
   D. That he is very physically unattractive

4. In Greece a downward nod means 'yes'. An upward nod means 'no'. What other gesture is used in Greece to say 'yes'?
   A. Thumb up finger point
   B. Tilting head side to side
   C. Touching your nose
   D. Clapping your hands

5. Irish people use the 'OK' sign to tell each other everything is fine. What would a Kuwaiti understand by this gesture?
   A. You're saying they've no love in their heart
   B. You're saying they are stupid
   C. You're giving them the 'evil eye'
   D. You're saying you have no money

6. How do you gesture for someone to come to you in Japan?
   A. Palm down hand movement
   B. Palm up hand movement
   C. Clenching your teeth
   D. Eye touch

7. Match the meaning of sticking out your tongue with the 'culture'?
   A. Ireland   1. Aggression
   B. Tibet   2. A childish insult
   C. Pacific Islands 3. Joking/Flirting
   D. Texting   4. Welcome/Respect

8. The 'V' sign usually means 'peace/victory'. In Ireland (with the back of the hand pointing outwards), what does it mean?
   A. To propose marriage to you
   B. To ask you for help
   C. To invite you for dinner
   D. To insult you

a. **Do you know any other gestures from around the world?**
b. **Demonstrate one typical gesture from your country.**

PART 2A NON-VERBAL COMMUNICATION

GREETINGS: Which of the ways in the box do you use to greet someone in your country? (Does it depend on if it's a formal/informal situation/between two males or two females etc?)

A. Kiss on the cheeks *B. Shake hands* *C. Embrace* *D. Bow* *E. Nod* *F. Other*

1. Which of the ways in the box do you think Irish people generally use to greet each other?
2. TASK: Say hello like you're Irish. *Nod your head (sideways or upwards), click your tongue, smile or wink and say 'Howya', 'Well' or 'How's it goin'?'* (Try it on an Irish person.)

TOUCH: From the box, write down one situation in which each form of physical contact would be appropriate or inappropriate in your culture? Work individually and share back with the class.

A. Hold hands *B. Link arms* *C. High fives* *D. Arm around shoulder* *E. Pat on head*

3. Do you think these 'rules' of physical contact are different in other cultures? (*It might depend on social context, relationship of the people, gender, age etc.*)
4. Do you think people use a lot of physical contact in Ireland? Do Irish generally touch more or less than in your culture?

INTERPERSONAL DISTANCE: We all have a sense of 'comfortable' distance between us and another person when we're speaking. If the person is too close, we'll back away and vice versa.

5. 'Comfortable' distance depends on the situation. Match the distances to the situations below.

INTERPERSONAL DISTANCE (Ireland)	Intimate (0-45cm)	Personal (45-80cm)	Social (80-300cm)	Public (3m +)

Example Situations	*A. Talking with classmates* *B. Date with your boy/girlfriend* *C. Business presentation* *D. Chatting with family*

6. TASK: Find the 'comfortable' social distance with students of different nationalities in your class. Does the distance change if you imagine the other student is your boss/boyfriend or girlfriend/teacher etc?
7. Which countries do you think have smaller or larger interpersonal distance? Do Irish stand closer/further away compared to your country?

IRISH PEOPLE: Is it possible to recognise nationality from how people move? Give an example.

8. How have **'Ireland's history with England'** and **'the weather'** affected how Irish people move? Try to explain the body movements below.

INFLUENCE	HISTORY WITH ENGLAND	THE WEATHER
IRISH BODY MOVEMENT	*- Wink a lot and nudge each other* *- Sometimes talk through the side of the mouth*	*- Don't use hand gestures a lot* *- Shrug shoulders a lot* *- Walk quickly*

viii. Can you demonstrate some typical movement from your country? (What might have influenced this?)

PART 2B HOW IRISH SOUND – INTERJECTIONS

1. ONLINE SECTION – AUDIO 8.2B.1 – Listen and match the interjection sounds with their meanings below.

Yay! -- Sshh -- Phew -- Pew -- Huh? -- Argh -- Yuck -- Awww (tch) -- Aha. aha -- Ouch -- Oh? -- Brrr -- Oops
Tch tch tch -- Mwah -- Aah. OK -- Hmmm -- Grrr -- Uh oh -- HaHa -- Blah blah -- Meh -- Em/eh/um -- Mmmm

Surprise		I understand		Be quiet		I don't approve	
Pain		Pausing		I'm happy		Smells bad	
Relief		We're in trouble		Frustration		My mistake	
A kiss		I'm thinking		I don't understand		I'm cold	
I'm angry		That's funny		Tastes good		Sympathy	
It's not very good		I'm not listening		Tastes bad		I'm listening	

2. Respond to different situations using some of the interjections above. (Your teacher can give you some examples.)
3. Can you think of any interjections you use in your language that are different from the ones above?
4. AUDIO 8.2B.2 – What do these typical Irish interjections mean? – **Wha'? Hah? Ah shur. Inbreath affirmation.**

PART 3 DANCE LIKE NOBODY IS WATCHING

ADJECTIVES

Elegant - Energetic - Athletic
Fun - Powerful - Rhythmical
Passionate - Serious
Theatrical - Sensual
Sophisticated - Intimate
Emotional - Funny - Seductive
Intense - Beautiful
Graceful - Delicate
Joyful - Formal - Competitive
Traditional - Romantic
Improvised - Classical
Modern - Tribal - Expressive
Informal - Cool - Acrobatic

1. Match the pictures with the dances in the grid below.
2. Choose two adjectives from above for each dance or choose your own adjectives.
3. Watch footage of each dance. See ONLINE SECTION. Which is your favourite? Why?
4. What adjectives would you use to describe how you dance? (Do you dance 'like nobody is watching'?)

DANCE	PICTURE	ADJECTIVE	DANCE	PICTURE	ADJECTIVE
Breakdance (USA)			Disco (USA)		
Samba (Brazil)			Gangnam (South Korea)		
Ballet (Russia)			Tango (Argentina)		
Haka (New Zealand)			Cossack (Ukraine)		
Bharatanatyam (India)			Flamenco (Spain)		
Dragon dance (China)			Adumu (Kenya)		
Kabuki (Japan)			Waltz (Austria)		
Belly Dance (Turkey)			CanCan (France)		

PART 4 WHAT TYPE OF ENGLISH LANGUAGE LEARNER ARE YOU?

1. How do you remember. for example. a phone number? Do you see it? Hear it? Imagine typing it on your phone?
2. Do each task below and rate each from 1 (almost impossible) to 9 (really easy) for you. Get the three Totals.

VISUAL - SEE...	1-9	AUDITORY - HEAR...	1-9	KINAESTHETIC - FEEL...	1-9
The colour of the school front door		Your friend with the softest voice		Jumping off a metre high wall	
Your friend with the longest hair		Church bells in the distance		Holding a smooth. heavy stone	
The biggest book in your house		A car starting on a cold day		Your fingers in cold water	
A childhood teacher's face		Your voice under water		Caressing a cat or dog	
The stripes on a tiger		A childhood friend's voice		Putting on a pair of wet socks	
TOTAL		TOTAL		TOTAL	

3. Which 'sense' scores the highest for you? How do think this might affect how you study/learn a language?

PART 5 IRISH DANCING

1. What type of art forms do you think are most important in your country's culture? Are visual arts (painting etc), auditory (music) or kinaesthetic (dance) strongest?
2. Does being a good dancer have a high status in your culture? What dance is most associated with your country? Can you demonstrate it now?
3. It has been said that 'Irish people are a very musical people but not really great movers.' What do you think this means? (Would you agree?)
4. Read the information below and answer the questions about Irish dancing.

1. How did the meaning of Irish dancing change?	3. What parts of the dancers' bodies hardly move?
2. Who wears soft shoes in Irish dancing?	4. Name three types of Irish dances

HISTORY: *In early Celtic times, Irish people used to dance circular ritual dances to honour their pagan gods. Over time, these developed into social events. The dances began to have fixed moves and rhythms. Group dances were taught by 'dance masters' who travelled around Ireland. In the 19th century, dancing at the crossroads on summer evenings in local communities was a popular rural activity. Nowadays, these traditional dances are still a common sight at social events like weddings and festivals. There are also competitions called 'feiseanna' where the best dancers compete.*

THE CLOTHES: *Two types of shoes are worn in Irish dancing: hard and soft. The hard shoes are similar to tap shoes, with the toes and heels made of fibreglass. The soft shoes are like a ballet shoe and are only worn by women. Women wear traditional dresses and curl their hair. The men wear shirts and trousers.*

THE DANCE: *Irish dancing has very quick, precise leg movements but the body and arms stay straight and stationary. People usually dance in square formations, often involving two sets of couples. There are three basic types of Irish dances - jigs, reels and hornpipes. The jig is the most common with the most basic step to a rhythm of '**one** two three, **one** two three'.*

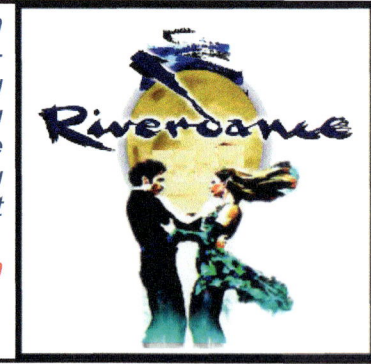

5. Watch some video of Irish dancing. SEE ONLINE SECTION. Which of the adjectives on the previous page would you use to describe Irish dancing?
6. Look carefully at the 'one two three' Irish dance step in the ONLINE SECTION. Can you do it? Try!
   One of the most popular group dances is 'The Walls of Limerick'. Can you do it as a class?
7. Can you write a short history, similar to the one above, of dance in your country?

RIVERDANCE: *In 1994, Irish dancing wasn't famous outside of Ireland and even in Ireland it was seen as quite old-fashioned and unfashionable. This all changed, however, with a seven-minute performance of Riverdance during the interval in the song contest, the Eurovision. The performance was seen all across Europe and Irish dancing was about to become famous around the world. The Riverdance show has become the most successful music and dance show ever to come from Ireland. It has been touring since 1995 and it has been seen live by over twenty million people in thirty different countries.*
a. *Watch 'Riverdance at the Eurovision'. (SEE ONLINE SECTION.) Do you like it? Can you understand why the show became such a success?*
b. *Is your country's traditional dance known around the world? Should it be?*

ON YOUR OWN

1. **PHYSICAL GAMES: Mirror Movements** – In pairs, face a partner and copy their momvements. **Charades** – Mime action words. **Spell words physically** – Split into two groups. A group of six people must make a word with six letters etc. Each student makes one letter with their body. The other group must read the word. **Have a 'dance off'.**
2. **Statue Dancing** – Hold your body without moving in a pose or position from one of the dances from PART 3 (or another dance). The other students must guess what dance it is.
3. **Image Theatre. 1.** Individually, make a body position that signifies a feeling – anger/happiness etc. The others must guess what feeling you are representing. **2.** In groups, one director will create a scene placing the students/actors in a different positions. Actors don't move. The audience must look at the scene and comment on what they think is happening. **3.** Act out a scene without words. The audience must watch and guess what is happening.
4. Go watch Irish dancing. Join in. (The most important attribute to start in Irish dancing is just enthusiasm!)

WARM UP

1. What is your favourite film? Why do you like it?
2. Have you ever been really scared watching a film?
3. Have you ever cried watching a film?
4. Name one film that always makes you laugh.
5. Have you ever seen any Irish films or films about Ireland?

PART 1 IRISH ACTORS

1. Match the Irish Hollywood actors and the characters they play with the film each appears in and the pictures below.

ACTOR & CHARACTER	FILM	PICTURE
James Nesbitt – 'Bofor'		
Maureen O'Hara – 'Doris Walker'		
Brendan Gleeson – 'Mad Eye Moody'		
Michael Fassbender – 'Magneto'		
Gabriel Byrne – 'D'Artagnan'		
Richard Harris – 'Marcus Aurelius'		
Domhnall Gleeson – 'General Hux'		
Liam Neeson – 'Oskar Schindler'		
Colin Farrell – 'Alexander the Great'		
A. Schindler's List **B.** X-Men **C.** Miracle on 34th Street **D.** The Hobbit **E.** Gladiator **F.** Alexander **G.** The Man in the Iron Mask **H.** Harry Potter **I.** Star Wars		

2. Do you know any of the actors/actresses above? Who are the most famous actors/actresses from your country?
3. Who is your favourite actor/actress? Why do you like them? What makes them so good?
4. Imagine you are interviewing your favourite actor/actress. Prepare questions to ask and role-play the interview.

Co. Wicklow, Ireland

Cillin Chaoimhin HOLLYWOOD

The Original

PART 2A IRISH MOVIES

1. Match the Irish films below with the correct genre and description. Use the film covers to help you.

IRISH FILMS	GENRES	DESCRIPTIONS
i. In the Name of the Father	**1.** Musical	**A.** *'A young woman whose husband has died discovers that he has left her ten messages to help her start a new life.'*
ii. Once	**2.** True Story	**B.** *'During the Irish War of Independence, two brothers fight in a guerrilla war against the British forces.'*
iii. The Guard	**3.** Love Story	**C.** *'A Dublin street musician and a Czech girl write and record songs that tell their love story.'*
iv. His & Hers	**4.** Animation	**D.** *'An Irishman in England is arrested for being involved in an IRA bombing and both he and his father wrongly go to prison.'*
v. Into the West	**5.** Historical Drama	**E.** *'Ben, a young Irish boy and his sister Saoirse, who can change into a seal, try to free the faeries and save the spirit world.'*
vi. P.S. I love you	**6.** Documentary	**F.** *'Different Irish women, from young to very old, talk about their relationships with the men in their lives.'*
vii. Song of the Sea	**7.** Action Comedy	**G.** *'Grandpa Ward gives a horse to his grandchildren. When the horse is stolen, the two boys travel across Ireland to try find it.'*
viii. The Wind that Shakes the Barley	**8.** Family Adventure	**H.** *'An unusual Irish policeman and a follow-the-rules American FBI agent investigate international drug smugglers.'*

Film	Genre	Description
i.		
ii.		
iii.		
iv.		
v.		
vi.		
vii.		
viii.		

2. Have you seen any of the films before?
   Watch the trailers for any of the ones you haven't seen in the ONLINE SECTION. Which of the films would you most like to watch? Why?

PART 2B GENRES & DESCRIPTIONS

1. Think of a film for each genre below. Which type of film is your favourite? Can you think of any other genres?

   > *1. Science Fiction 2. Romantic Comedy 3. Thriller 4. Western*
   > *5. Fantasy 6. Horror 7. War 8. Children's*

2. Can you identify the film below from the description?

   > *The legendary story of a 13th century hero whose wife is killed by English soldiers and who leads the Scottish against the English king and his army in a fight for 'Freedom!' (Directed by Mel Gibson)*

3. Write a short description for a film you like. Get other students to guess the film and/or say what genre it is.

PART 3 NATIONAL CINEMA

1. From the Irish films you've seen, or from your general knowledge of Irish culture, what would you expect a 'typical' Irish film to look like? What would the typical subject matter or focus be? What can you say about the language, dress and behaviour of the characters?

On the left are two examples of films which might be said to contain some typical elements of Irish cinema.

1. **BLOODY SUNDAY** is a film about a real political event that took place in Northern Ireland in 1972.
   Many Irish films deal with the subject of Ireland's historical and political relationship with England.
2. **INTERMISSION** is a crime drama but with plenty of humour and a focus on human relationships.
   Irish films dealing with serious issues often contain large elements of comedy, reflecting the strong Irish sense of humour.

Which three films on the previous page would fit best into either of the two categories above? How would you describe the subject matter of the other Irish films on the previous page?

2. Can you match the national cinema descriptions below with the correct country?

> **A.** *Includes lots of songs and dancing in unexpected places, melodrama and humour.*
> **B.** *Martial arts, adult animation, monster films and horror.*
> **C.** *Big blockbuster films with lots of action and visually impressive special effects.*
> **D.** *Naturalistic films about normal people, also dealing with social limitations, especially of women.*
> **E.** *Artistic, romantic, philosophical films, often reflecting a director's personal creative vision.*

JAPAN	IRAN	INDIA	FRANCE	USA

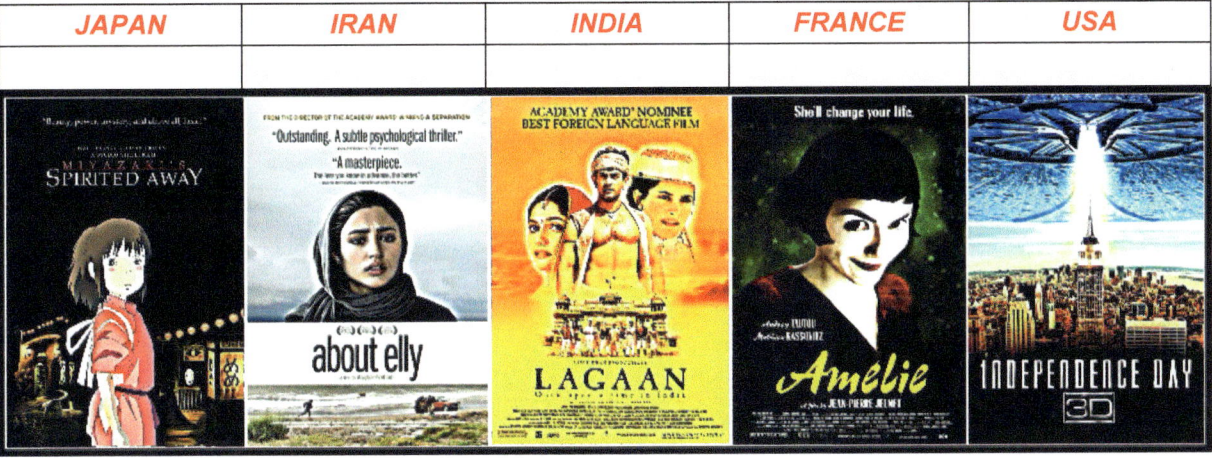

3. If your country is included, do you agree with the national cinema description above?
4. If your country is not included, how would you describe your country's national cinema? What are 'typical' films from your country about? What genres are most popular? What do they look like? Etc.
   Can you write a short description, similar to above (or in PART 2A), for a typical film from your country?
5. Do you like films from your own country? Why? Why not?

PART 4 FILM PLOTS

1. Can you recognise two well-known films from the questions about the plots? (Can you answer the questions?)

FILM A:	FILM B:
1. Where were they going?	1. What was the world called?
2. Why were they so confident about going so fast?	2. What physical problem did the man have?
3. Why was it hard for the young man and woman to be together?	3. How did the man enter the other world?
4. What went wrong with the ship?	4. Why did his opinions start to change?
5. Why did so many people die?	5. Who did he fall in love with?
6. How did the young woman survive?	6. Which side did he fight on?

2. Write your own plot questions for a film you like and get other students to try guess what the film is.
3. **TASK:** Write a typical plot for a film from your own country.

UNIT 9 IRISH FILM

PART 5A HOLLYWOOD HORROR FILMS

Movies are not exactly like real life. There are certain clichés or plot 'shortcuts' we often see in Hollywood movies. For example, in horror movies, if a character is specifically told not to do something, they'll do exactly that… usually with very bad consequences. We're all familiar with that moment when you know for sure a character in a horror movie is going to die in the next scene. If only characters followed some simple survival rules…

1.   For each of the examples below, say whether it is a good idea or a bad idea, **Do** or **Don't**.

HOW TO SURVIVE A HORROR MOVIE	Do	Don't
Tell the group you will 'be right back'.		
When searching a house for danger at night, turn on a light.		
If the electricity goes off, search the basement room under the house.		
Check the back seat of your car before you get in.		
Listen to the soundtrack. If the music gets faster when you open a door, close it.		
Listen to all warnings from children or animals about danger that is coming.		
After killing the monster/murderer, turn your back without checking they're really dead.		
Publicly announce your big plans for the future if you survive.		

2.   In pairs or small groups can you think of any advice for 'How to survive a war/disaster/action movie' or 'How to get the boy/girl you love in a romantic comedy'? Etc.

PART 5B HOLLYWOOD MOVIE CLICHÉS

1.   Can you match the titles in the grid with the movie clichés below from different types of films?

Sleep well		You do love me!	
Phone manners		Just in time	
Get the bus instead?		Solving a case	
Wait your turn		Too cool to watch	

A. Never say goodbye when you hang up. However, keep saying hello to a dead dial tone.

B. A character is offered a dream job in another city but gives it up to stay with his/her love interest.

C. If you're in danger, the car won't start first time. If it falls off a cliff, it will always explode.

D. If a character wakes from a nightmare, he/she sits straight up in bed, sweating and breathing heavily.

E. All bombs have a big clock to say when they'll explode. The hero will disarm it with one second left.

F. When the hero destroys something in a spectacular explosion, he walks away without looking back.

G. In martial arts films, when the hero fights a group of bad guys, they will only attack one-at-a-time.

H. A detective will always be suspended from duty by his police chief before he can catch the criminal.

2.   In pairs/small groups, can you add any more Movie Clichés to the list above?

3.   **MOVIE STEREOTYPES.** In Hollywood films, there can also be clichés of national stereotype. For example, Irish characters in Hollywood films often tend to be policemen, priests or drunken writers. They also seem to like fighting and, depending on the type of film, might even believe in fairies and Leprechauns. *Are there any Hollywood stereotypes of people from your country? Are they positive or negative?*

ON YOUR OWN – AND THE OSCAR GOES TO…

1.   Listen to different types of instrumental music. Close your eyes. Imagine the music as the soundtrack to different scenes from a film you're creating. Open your eyes. Share the scenes with your class.

2.   Think of a real event from your life. Create a film story board of the event with drawings and dialogue. Using other students as actors, take photos of them acting out the incident. Add them to the story board.

3.   Imagine you now have to sell/promote your new film to a film studio. Make a presentation to your class.

4.   Imagine you are a film critic. Write a review of a film you have seen recently for your local newspaper.

5.   Make your own short films and have an Oscar night with prizes for Best Film/Best Actor etc.

WARM UP

1. What was your favourite/least favourite subject in school?
2. Did you like history in school? Did you learn about the history and cultures of other countries or just your country?
3. How is history relevant in your life now?
4. Talk about one important historical event in your country.

PART 1 CULTURAL DIFFERENCES

1. Can you match the cultural advice given by local people with the country from around the world and the reasons below?

CULTURAL ADVICE	COUNTRY	REASON
Don't whistle at night - Fai		
Have your birthday party on Thursday instead of Saturday - Mido		
Don't joke in a business meeting - Ralf		
Don't eat tacos with a knife and fork - Frida		
Don't smile too much - Yana		
Don't make the OK hand gesture - Luana		
Be happy if I say you look fat - Sun		
Say hello to a magpie bird if you see one on its own - Niall		
Don't plan anything important for Tuesday the 13th - Rafa		

COUNTRY
A. Germany **B.** Ireland **C.** China **D.** Russia **E.** Egypt **F.** Spain **G.** Mexico **H.** Brazil **I.** Thailand

REASON
1. This is not the appropriate moment for this
2. You will avoid bad luck
3. This is better for people who are working the next day
4. People will be suspicious of you if they don't know you
5. In most places this is good but here it is insulting
6. Be careful, you might call a ghost
7. This means that we are friends and comfortable together
8. This date is associated with bad luck
9. People will think you look snobby or ridiculous

2. What cultural advice would you give to someone visiting your country for the first time?
3. What advice would you give someone visiting Ireland?
   (For example, if someone asked you what clothes to bring with them to Ireland, what would you suggest? Etc.)

QUOTES

Which is your favourite quote? Why?

"A nation's culture lives in the hearts & soul of its people." – Mahatma Gandhi

"People without knowledge of their history & culture are a tree without roots."
    – Marcus Garvey

"Culture is like a body's immune system. Like a body dealing with an infection, a group enforces its rules, either actively or passively." – Henry Cloud

"Without memory, there is no culture, no society." – Elie Wiesel

"Preserving our own culture does not mean disrespecting others."
    – Cesar Chavez

"Debate & different views make our culture richer."– Ibrahim Babangida

"Language is the key to the heart of a culture."– Ahmed Deedat

"There is very little 'of course' when it comes to different cultures."
    – Janet Kagan

"The culture you are born in is just one reality. Other cultures are not failed efforts at being like you. They are equally unique & valid." – Wade Davis

"Individual cultures are good but they don't replace the universal experiences like love, crying & laughter common to all." – Aberjhani

Share your genuine feelings about the quotes... join the discussion. Can you share any similar quotes from your own culture?

HMM, I'M NOT SURE IF HE WAS REALLY BEING FRIENDLY...

...OR WAS IT JUST CULTURAL?

UNIT 10 IRISH CULTURE AND HISTORY

PART 2 HISTORY ALL AROUND US

In Ireland, like any country, historical events have had a big impact on the development of the people and their culture. If we look carefully at a society, we can see the effects of history all around us.

Using your imagination and any knowledge you have of Ireland, what historical reasons can you think of for the following things that you might notice around you in Ireland today?

1. Ireland is an island surrounded by seas full of some of the best fishing in the world…
   Why don't the Irish eat a lot of fish?

2. The west of Ireland is famous for its stone walls. They are a beautiful part of the countryside…
   Who built them in the 19th century and why?

3. Over seven million tourists visit Ireland every year. In surveys, Ireland often comes in the Top Ten countries in the world for friendliness and being welcoming to strangers…
   Why are the Irish generally seen as so friendly and welcoming to visitors? (Is this your experience?) What do you think are the top reasons visitors give for coming to Ireland?

4. There are no snakes in Ireland. Legend says that Saint Patrick forced them to leave...
   What geological reasons can you think of for Ireland's lack of snakes? (Britain has snakes.)

PART 2 HISTORY ALL AROUND US *contd.*

5. It has been said about the Irish that they make 'great diplomats but terrible politicians'…
   What do you think this means? What does it say about the character of Irish people?

6. In international football, your country might play against either Northern Ireland or the Republic of Ireland. However, in rugby, you would only play against Ireland…
   Why do you think the island of Ireland has two football teams but only one rugby team? And what anthem or song is played before games involving each of the teams?

7. In 1840, the population of the island of Ireland was about 8.5 million. By the end of the 20th century, it had dropped to about 5.5 million. By 2015, it was rising again to nearly 6.5 million…
   Why did Ireland's population fall so much from 1840 to 2000? And why does Ireland have a much higher birthrate than most of the rest of Europe now?

8. Gránuaile (Grace O'Malley) was a pirate queen in the 16th century in the west of Ireland. She was the most famous, powerful leader in the history of the O'Malley clan…
   What historical/cultural reasons can you think of for why Irish women, to this day, have traditionally been very independent and had strong roles in society?

PART 2 HISTORY ALL AROUND US *contd.*

9. An Irish passport is ranked in the Top Ten in the world…
    What reasons can you think of for why an Irish passport is such a good one to have?

    [ ]

10. Lots of American multinational companies (*Google, Apple, IBM, Facebook, Pfizer* etc.) have their European base and headquarters in Ireland…
    Why is Ireland an attractive location for so many American multinational companies?

    [ ]

11. You will sometimes see Irish people on holiday with very red skin from the sun…
    Why do Irish people sometimes stay out too long in the sun on holiday? How might the Irish weather make people good at living in the moment but bad at planning?

    [ ]

12. In the south of Ireland, the majority of people (roughly 85%) identify themselves as of Catholic religion. In the north, the majority is Protestant (48-50% Protestant/45% Catholic)…
    What historical reasons can you think of for this difference between North and South? And how do you think the border came into existence as it is today?

    [ ]

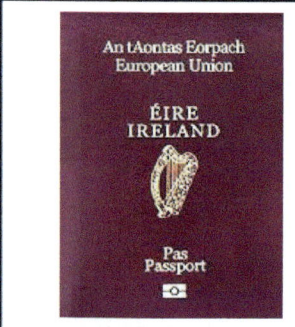  

ON YOUR OWN

1. Which of the questions do you find the most interesting?
2. Think of similar questions you could ask about your own country and ask them to the rest of your class.

UNIT 11 IRISH FESTIVALS & SOCIAL LIFE

WARM UP

1. What would be your perfect way to celebrate your birthday - going out to club/a meal in a restaurant/something else?
2. How do people generally socialise in your country? Do people drink in your country when they go out?
3. What is your favourite (alcoholic or non-alcoholic) drink?
4. Have you been on a night out in Ireland? Is socialising in Ireland very different from in your country?

PART 1 WORLD FESTIVALS

1. Match the pictures with a festival and 'what you do' at each.

FESTIVAL	PICTURE	WHAT YOU DO
Carnival - Brazil		
Oktoberfest - Germany		
Ice Sculpting Festival - China		
Lantern Festival - Taiwan		
White Nights Festival - Russia		
Burning Man - USA		
Water Festival - Thailand		
Bull running - Spain		
Dia de los Muertos - Mexico		

A. Be ready to get wet **B.** Look up! **C.** Just express yourself
D. Remember the dead **E.** Dance on the streets **F.** Run fast!
G. Wear gloves **H.** Drink beer **I.** Celebrate fireworks & history

2. Have you been to any of these festivals? Which would you most like to go to? Is there any other festival you'd like to go to?
3. What's the best festival you've ever been to?
4. What are the most famous festivals in your country? How do you celebrate them?

Share your genuine feelings about the quotes... join the discussion. Can you share any similar quotes from your own culture?

Hungry?
We have food.
Thirsty?
We have alcohol.
Lonely?
We have alcohol.

IRISH PUB SIGN

PART 2A IRISH FESTIVALS

1. On which date is each festival? Match the festivals with the traditions they're associated with below.

FESTIVAL	DATE	TRADITION	FESTIVAL	DATE	TRADITION
Christmas Day			Shrove Tuesday		
St. Patrick's Day			Halloween		
Easter			St. Valentine's Day		
New Year's Eve			April Fools' Day		

TRADITION	A. Play a joke B. Eat chocolate C. Send a card secretly to someone you like D. Eat turkey E. Wear a scary costume F. Eat pancakes G. Sing 'Auld Lang Syne' H. Wear a shamrock

2. Which of the festivals do you celebrate in your country? How do you celebrate them?

PART 2B IRISH FESTIVALS - HALLOWEEN

1. The modern Halloween comes from an old Irish festival called *Samhain*. In ancient Celtic Ireland, the end of October was celebrated as the beginning of winter and a time for remembering the dead. We still practice many of the old festival's traditions.
Can you match the modern Halloween traditions to their original meanings below?

TRADITION	MEANING
1. Light big outdoor bonfires	A. To help you have a baby in year ahead
2. Wear a mask	B. To help the poor celebrate
3. Trick or Treat - ask for food/money at people's houses	C. To scare away evil spirits
4. Bob for apples - bite an apple in a basin of water	D. To guide your soul in the next world
5. Jack-O-Lantern - put a light inside a 'pumpkin head'	E. To confuse evil spirits if you meet them

2. A big part of Halloween is about being scared - telling scary stories, watching horror films etc. What are the scariest stories/monsters in your culture? Why do you think we like to feel scared?

3. Another Irish Halloween tradition is the eating of *barmbrack*, a bread-like fruitcake. Inside a *barmbrack*, you will find a few surprises. What would each one mean if you got it in your slice of cake?

OBJECT IN CAKE	MEANING	
1. A piece of cloth	A. You will get married soon	
2. A ring	B. You'll have an argument with somebody	
3. A stick	C. You will not get married this year	
4. A pea	D. You will have money this year	
5. A coin	E. You will be poor this year	

4. Are there any superstitions of good/bad luck in your culture for getting married, making money etc?

PART 2C IRISH FESTIVALS - ST. PATRICK'S DAY

Read **four suprising facts** about St. Patrick's Day and then look at the questions below.

St. Patrick's Day celebrates everything Irish... but Patrick wasn't born in Ireland	Patrick is Ireland's patron saint... but St. Patrick's Day is not really a religious celebration
St. Patrick's colour was blue not green	The first St. Patrick's Day parade wasn't in Ireland

1. St. Patrick is celebrated for bringing Christianity to Ireland in the 5th century AD. What religion were the Irish before he came? (Bonus Question: how did Patrick use the **shamrock** to explain Christianity to the Irish?)

2. Why did Patrick first come to Ireland? | As a tourist -- As a slave -- For love -- As part of an invading army |

3. Why do you think religion and specifically the Catholic religion became so important in Irish cultural identity that St. Patrick's Day became unofficially Ireland's national day?

4. Why do you think green became the colour of St. Patrick's Day. and Ireland in general. rather than blue?

5. The first St. Patrick's Day parade was in Boston in 1737. Who do you think started the parades there?

A. Is there a national day in your country? Can you make four facts about it?

B. What is your country's colour? (The colour your sports teams play in etc.) Do you know why this colour is used?

C. In Ireland. alcohol sales more than double on St. Patrick's Day. Is alcohol important in celebration in your country?

PART 3A DRINKS AROUND THE WORLD

1. In pairs, can you match the different national drinks with the information and countries below?

1	2	3	4	5	6	7	8	9
Sake	Mate	Champagne	Port	Vodka	Tej	Tequila	Raki	Sangria

*A fruity summer drink - **Spain***		*Drunk at the end of a meal. Named after a region in the country - **Portugal***	
*Homemade honey wine - **Ethiopia***		*Non-alcoholic. Shared among friends - **Argentina***	
*Drink it to celebrate - **France***		*Made from rice. Never pour for yourself - **Japan***	
*Strong alcohol. Make a toast - **Russia***		*Sometimes drunk with salt & lemon but not drunk with a worm - **Mexico***	
*Clear drink that turns milky when you add water or ice - **Turkey***			

2. Have you tried any of the drinks? Choose one and find out more about how/why/when it is drunk.
3. What is your country's national drink? Do you like it? Is there any ritual associated with drinking it?

PART 3B IRISH DRINKS

1. Match these typical Irish drinks to the occasions people drink them.

1	2	3	4	5	6

Picture	Drink	Occasion
1		
2		
3		
4		
5		
6		

DRINK	OCCASION
i. Cider ii. Red lemonade iii. Guinness iv. Poitín v. Irish coffee vi. Hot whiskey	***A.** Have a pint in the pub **B.** More popular in the summer **C.** Drink carefully (high alcohol & it used to be illegal) **D.** At Christmas **E.** When you're sick with a cold **F.** Popular at children's parties*

2. Find out more about one of the drinks above. Would you associate any other drink with Ireland?
3. Are different drinks associated with different occasions in your culture? Tell your class about them.
4. If you have experience of socialising in Ireland, which statement below would you agree with more?

The social scene is one of the best things about Ireland	*Ireland's drinking culture is a problem*

PART 4A THE IRISH PUB

The pub is at the centre of Irish social life. It is a place to escape life's problems and a place with its own customs.

1. Why go to the pub? In pairs, choose from the box the things you think Irish people **do** or **don't do** in a pub.

A. Listen to live music B. Heart-to-heart talk with friend C. Do business D. Go on first date E. Have drink with boss & workmates F. Dance G. Tell stories/gossip H. Watch sport I. Play music J. Have lunch K. Make life plans L. Read paper

2. The 'Irish pub' has been exported around the world. What do you think makes Irish pubs special? Is it exportable?

THE ROUNDS SYSTEM

3. The 'rounds system' is based on the principle that when someone buys you a drink, you buy one back. Can you explain the three statements below?
   a. It's impossible for two Irish people to go for one drink.
   b. The 'rounds system' may appear to be very casual but it definitely isn't.
   c. Buying a round or buying someone a pint is not about money, it's something deeper with symbolic meaning.
4. Do you think 'rounds' is a good or bad system? Is there any similar system in your country?

PART 4B CHEERS AROUND THE WORLD

1. 'Cheers' in different languages - how many in the box do you know?

German		Japanese	
Swedish		Arabic	
Zulu		Lithuanian	
Italian		Polish	
Irish		Hebrew	

2. SLÁINTE
1. Oogy wawa
3. Prost
4. Skål
5. Cin Cin
6. I sveikata
7. Kanpai
8. L'Chaim
9. Fe Sahetek
10. NA ZDROWIE

2. How do you say it in your language (if not included in the box)?
4. What would you typically 'toast to' in your country?

PART 5 DINNER PARTY - WHAT DO YOU SAY?

1. IN YOUR COUNTRY: Imagine you've invited some friends to a dinner in your house - *What would you cook? What time would you eat? What would you have to drink? Would your guests bring anything?*
2. IN IRELAND: Hospitality is central to Irish culture. If you invite people to your home, it's important to say the right things to make them feel welcome. So... As your guests arrive below for your dinner party, work in groups and decide what you might say in each moment. (The first one is done as an example.)

A. The doorbell rings. You open the door...	E. Everyone is sitting at the table ready to eat...
Hi, how are you? - How's it going? - What's the story? - Great to see you - Thanks for coming Long time, no see - Come on in etc.	
B. You offer to take your guests' coats...	F. You invite them to have more food...
C. You tell them to go join the party...	G. You offer more drinks...
D. You offer them a drink before dinner...	H. You say goodbye at the end of the night...

3. **NOW IMAGINE YOU ARE A <u>GUEST</u> AT THE DINNER PARTY**
   i. The dinner party is at 7pm. What time should you arrive?
   ii. What (if anything) should you bring with you?
   iii. What topics should you generally talk about? Are there any topics you shouldn't talk about?
   iv. What would you say if...

A. Your host offers you a drink but you don't drink alcohol **B.** *You want to say you like the food*
C. Your host offers you some more food but you don't want any more
D. You want to go to the toilet *E. You want to say goodbye at the end of the night*

ON YOUR OWN

1. Go to a St. Patrick's Day parade. Go 'trick or treating' at Halloween. Go to a typical Irish festival like the Rose of Tralee. Lisdoonvarna, the Puck Fair or the Fleadh Cheoil. Report back.
2. In groups, invent your own festival. What will you celebrate? How? Etc. Share with the class.
3. Invent a new drink and prepare a marketing campaign for it. Present it to the class.
4. Have an international dinner party together. Everybody should bring some typical food or drink from their country.
5. Go out as a class and enjoy yourselves. Report back on your Irish nightlife experiences and adventures!

WARM UP

1. How popular is football in your country? Are you a fan? How big is the World Cup when your team plays?
2. Who is the most popular sportsperson in your country (past or present)? Why is he/she so popular?
3. Is there any person in your country who divides opinion, some people love and some really don't like him/her?

It is two weeks before the Korea & Japan World Cup, 2002. Ireland is getting ready... Match the adjectives/expressions below with how the fans, players or both might be feeling.

1. Stressed **2.** Excited **3.** Ready to party **4.** Under pressure
5. Relaxed **6.** Focused **7.** Nervous **8.** Ready to work hard
9. Looking forward to a holiday
10. Preparing mentally & physically for the challenge

PLAYERS	FANS	BOTH

PART 1 THE PREPARATION

1. Imagine you are responsible for organising the final World Cup preparations for the Ireland football team. Individually first, put the list below in order of importance from 1-10. Then compare with a partner.

WORLD CUP PREPARATIONS - Rank what is most important (1-10)	YOU	YOUR PARTNER
Correct footballs		
Relaxation		
Hard training		
Somewhere with sun & good weather		
A good quality football pitch		
A positive atmosphere among the players		
Isolation & protection away from media		
Correct medical & training equipment		
A good hotel		
As little travel stress as possible		

2. Mick McCarthy is Ireland's manager, Roy Keane is captain and Niall Quinn is the most experienced player. *(See next page.)* Who do you think is most responsible for making sure all the preparation is good - the manager, the captain, the players or the FAI (Irish football association)?
3. Ireland decide to prepare for the World Cup in Saipan. *(See map)* Why do you imagine Saipan was chosen?

Which is your favourite quote? Why?

"You discover more about a person in an hour of play than a year of talking." – Plato
"Be careful of men who are driven by rage. They are not in control of their own art or of themselves." – Henry Lawton
"Sometimes the best plan is to accept things & go with the flow." – Mark Bona
"Incompetence & stupid administration have always robbed Irish sport. There is a lack of ambition & expectation. I want a revolution." – Eamon Dunphy
"Lots of people confuse bad management with destiny." – Kim Hubbard
"As a coach, you need to trouble the comfortable & comfort the troubled." – Ric Charlesworth
"Why do anything unless it is going to be great?" – Peter Block
"The reasonable person adapts to the world, the unreasonable one tries to adapt the world to themselves. All progress depends on the unreasonable." – G.B. Shaw
"Leadership is based on inspiration not domination, on cooperation not intimidation." – William Arthur Ward
"Aggression is what I do. I go to war. You don't contest football matches in a reasonable state of mind." – Roy Keane

Share your genuine feelings about the quotes... join the discussion. Can you share any similar quotes from your own culture?

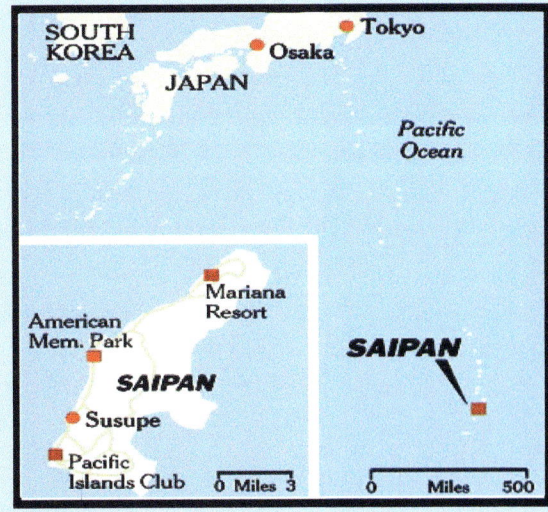

UNIT 12 IRISH FOOTBALL - SAIPAN

PART 2 THE MAIN CHARACTERS

1. Mick McCarthy, Roy Keane and Niall Quinn already had a long history together before 2002. **Read below.**

McCARTHY · KEANE · QUINN

In the 1990 World Cup in Italy, McCarthy was Ireland's captain. Quinn also played and scored. In 1992, Keane made his debut for Ireland, playing with McCarthy and Quinn. In 1993, McCarthy retired as a player. In 1994, Quinn and Keane qualified together for World Cup USA. In 1996, McCarthy became Ireland manager and in 1998 named Keane as captain. In 2000, Keane met McCarthy to discuss the need for better preparation, facilities etc. In 2001, Ireland eliminated Holland and qualified for the World Cup. Despite the joy among fans, players and management, Keane remained frustrated at poor Irish standards and mentality.

2. Can you see any possible complications/problems in the relationships between the three men?
3. Decide if the words/expressions describing each man is positive (+), negative (−) or neutral (N).

MICK McCARTHY	+/−/N
Loyal	
Direct	
Incompetent	
Decent	
Out of his depth	
Honest	
Straight-talking	

ROY KEANE	+/−/N
Perfectionist	
A Loner	
Outspoken	
Principled	
Volatile	
Demanding	
Passionate	

NIALL QUINN	+/−/N
Going with the flow	
Adaptable	
Uncaring	
Diplomatic	
Outgoing	
Upbeat	
A Yes-man	

PART 3 ARRIVAL IN SAIPAN

Ireland's trip to the World Cup is very badly organised. As the team travel for seventeen hours to Saipan via Holland, the Irish players joke that the FAI bought Holland's old plane tickets to get a discount. When the team arrives in Saipan, the football pitch is terrible. There are no footballs. The correct training and medical equipment haven't arrived.
Read the reactions of McCarthy, Keane and Quinn below and answer the questions.

Nothing has arrived – training gear, sun lotion, the official World Cup ball. The football pitch is really bad. I am annoyed. It makes me look bad in front of the players. Ultimately, preparation is my responsibility but someone in the FAI will have questions to answer over this. I know from looking at Roy that he's not happy. – McCARTHY

Things don't have to be perfect. This is a week of rest and relaxation. We don't have footballs or the right training gear but the skies are blue and the beach and hotel are great.. We're on our way to the World Cup. Relax. I know Roy is unhappy but I don't care. Human beings aren't an exact science. There is an indefinable thing called team spirit. – QUINN

We are Irish! The world loves us, we tell ourselves. We're at the World Cup to get the party started... Calm on one level. I am burning with anger on another level. I'm angry at the unprofessionalism, the lack of real ambition. This new fiasco eats into my soul. This is not what I've worked so hard for. You don't compromise on what you believe in. – KEANE

1. How do the reactions of the three men differ?	2. Who do you agree with most? How would you react?
3. What do you think each person should do next?	4. What do you think each person will do next?

PART 4 THE MEETING

In Saipan, Keane gives an interview to *The Irish Times* newspaper and is critical of the team's preparations. McCarthy is furious and organises a meeting of all the players. *Read the three accounts of the meeting below.*

I call a meeting. If someone has a problem, we will discuss it as a squad, not through the media. As the man in charge, I have to deal with Roy's newspaper article. I ask Roy, as captain, to explain to the group anything he is unhappy about. I hold up the article. Roy explodes. I've never seen a human being act like this before. The insults go on and on. He is out-of-control. Finally, I've had enough. I tell him to go and he storms out. Could I have done anything different? I don't think so. **- McCARTHY**

Mick stands in front of all the players. He takes out a copy of a newspaper article. 'Roy I want to speak to you about…' Bang! Suddenly, Roy goes off. For ten minutes it continues. It is an articulate, intelligent and complete destruction of Mick's character. All the players sit in silence, shocked. Afterwards, I wonder why I didn't try and stop Roy, why I didn't talk to him to get him to calm down. 'You have your excuse now. It's all my fault,' Roy shouts. Then, he's gone. The silence is as if a death has occurred in the room. **- QUINN**

Mick says, 'Roy, you seem unhappy about something.' Why is he doing this? Keep cool, I tell myself. 'You never wanted to play for your country,' he says. Suddenly, I snap. I don't hold back. It's everything. All the poor organisation over the years, disrespecting the Irish fans we're supposed to love. And I'm the captain of this crap. The other players know all this too. Any support? Quinny? Nothing. When I leave the room, I know McCarthy has got what he wants. He's humiliated me in front of my teammates. It was a trap. **- KEANE**

1. In what ways are the three accounts different?	**2.** What mistakes do you think each of them made?
3. Who do you feel most sympathy for?	**4.** What do you think will/should happen next?

PART 5 'A COUNTRY DIVIDED'

LISTENING A: Immediately after the meeting. McCarthy organises a press conference with Quinn beside him. McCarthy says he has sent Keane home. Back in Ireland, passions are high. Friends argue, grown men cry. The country is divided.

1. Listen and match each audio extract with a speaker below. *Audio File 12.5.a - ONLINE SECTION.*

AUDIO	SPEAKER	AUDIO	SPEAKER
1		5	
2		6	
3		7	
4		8	

A. Niall Quinn B. The psychologist C. The Irish Prime Minister D. The FAI representative (John Delaney) E. Mick McCarthy F. Keane's biographer (Eamon Dunphy) G. The Saipan pitch attendant H. Roy Keane

2. Listen to the audio again and answer the questions below.

i. McCarthy says he has sent Keane home for what reason?	ii. Who is Quinn worried about?
iii. Which two speakers agree that the football pitch in Saipan was really bad?	iv. Name one person who supports Keane and one who doesn't.
v. Why does the psychologist find the situation ironic?	vi. Who hopes for a resolution to the situation?

3. Are you hopeful of a resolution? Do you think it's possible for Keane to return? Would that be a good resolution?

PART 5 'A COUNTRY DIVIDED' *contd.*

LISTENING B: Nearly a week has passed. Quinn is working to try get Keane back to the team before the start of the World Cup. It is unclear if McCarthy will accept Keane back. Keane agrees to give a half-hour interview on Irish TV and it is thought that if he apologises, he will then be on a plane back to Japan.

i.   Listen to the audio of Keane, Quinn, McCarthy and the psychologist. Find out if Keane is coming back and then answer the questions below. **Audio File 12.5.b - ONLINE SECTION.**

1. What does Keane say is 'nonsense'?	**2.** How is Quinn feeling? Why is he feeling like this?
3. What is McCarthy hoping for?	**4.** Why does the psychologist think a phone call between Keane and McCarthy never happened?

PART 6 THE WORLD CUP

While Ireland play the World Cup. Keane is at home walking his dog. In the second round, Ireland are eliminated by Spain on penalties. Quinn and Keane announce their retirements from the Irish team. Among the fans, the arguments continue long after the World Cup even to this day…

So, whose side are you on?

PART 7 SAIPAN TO SUNDERLAND TO IRELAND AGAIN

1.   In pairs, say whether you think each of the events in the grid below is **TRUE** or **FALSE (T/F)**.

DATE	EVENT	T/F
Sept. '02	Keane, McCarthy and Quinn all release biographies. McCarthy's sells the best.	
Sept. '02	During a Sunderland v Manchester United game, Keane's ex-Irish teammate Jason McAteer makes fun of Keane about his book. Keane elbows McAteer in the head and gets a red card.	
Nov. '02	McCarthy quits as Ireland manager after fans sing Keane's name during a game.	
Apr. '04	With McCarthy gone, Keane returns to play for Ireland, to a mixed welcome.	
Nov. '05	Keane argues with his Manchester United manager and is forced to leave the club.	
Mar. '06	As Sunderland manager, McCarthy argues with his best player and loses his job.	
Aug. '06	Quinn buys Sunderland Football Club and the new manager he appoints is Keane.	
Apr. '07	As rival managers, Keane and McCarthy refuse to shake hands at a game against each other	
Jun. '12	Roy Keane's dog, Triggs, releases his autobiography. It sells very well.	
Nov. '13	Keane gets a job with the FAI. He is appointed Ireland's assistant manager.	
Jul. '16	With Keane as assistant manager, Ireland become European football champions.	

ON YOUR OWN

1.   Watch the Saipan documentary 'Red Mist' or read one of the autobiographies by Keane. Quinn or McCarthy.
2.   Read *The Irish Times* interview with Keane that caused all the trouble in Saipan. What do you think of it?
3.   Ask an Irish person what they thought of Saipan. Did they support McCarthy or Keane? Report back to the class.
4.   Write about a controversial incident in your country which divided public opinion.

THE IRISH CULTURE BOOK 2

Why is green the colour of Ireland? How have Irish inventions changed war, farming and football? Did St. Patrick really force all the snakes out of Ireland? Why are Irish people great diplomats but not such great politicians, great musicians but not such great dancers? Why don't we eat a lot of fish?

These are just some of the questions that are considered in this book. There are many more.

THE IRISH CULTURE BOOK 2 has three main aims:

- To help you find out about Irish culture
- To help you reflect on your own culture and build cross cultural awareness
- To help you enjoy practising your English

THE IRISH CULTURE BOOK consists of twelve units and covers a range of stimulating and thought-provoking topics connected to aspects of Irish culture. The units contain quotes, questions, exercises, authentic reading texts, listenings and links to online resources, as well as problem-solving activities. The discussions allow users to voice their own opinions, to think about Irish culture and by extension their own cultures.

The background notes in the TEACHER'S RESOURCE BOOK give clear instructions for every activity as well as extra information and talking points for the discussions, tapescripts and answer keys to the activities. The book can be used by teachers, by students as a self-access book or by anyone with an interest in exploring aspects of Irish culture in a learning or multicultural environment.

THE IRISH CULTURE BOOK 2 provides:

- Opportunities to discuss a variety of topics surrounding Irish culture
- Opportunities to practice speaking skills and fluency
- Motivating questions to engage high-level cognitive skills in English
- A range of interesting quotations on each topic
- Comparative exercises to foster further reflection and thought on other cultures
- Opportunities for follow-up spoken and written presentations
- Adaptable and stand-alone activities that can be used independently or as part of a structured course
- Easy-to-use format with clear explanatory notes and photocopiable materials in the RESOURCE BOOK
- Suggestions and links for a range of follow-on activities and discussions
- An 'On Your Own' section to promote continued learning and project work
- Regularly-updated Online Resources on THE IRISH CULTURE BOOK website

www.irishculturebook.com

Ian O'Malley has worked in ESL - in Ireland, Spain and Italy - since 1996. He has been a teacher, Academic Director and materials designer for language courses. He is an English language examiner and a teacher trainer of ESL teachers. He has an MA in English literature and is a previously published author.

ian@irishculturebook.com